AF487980

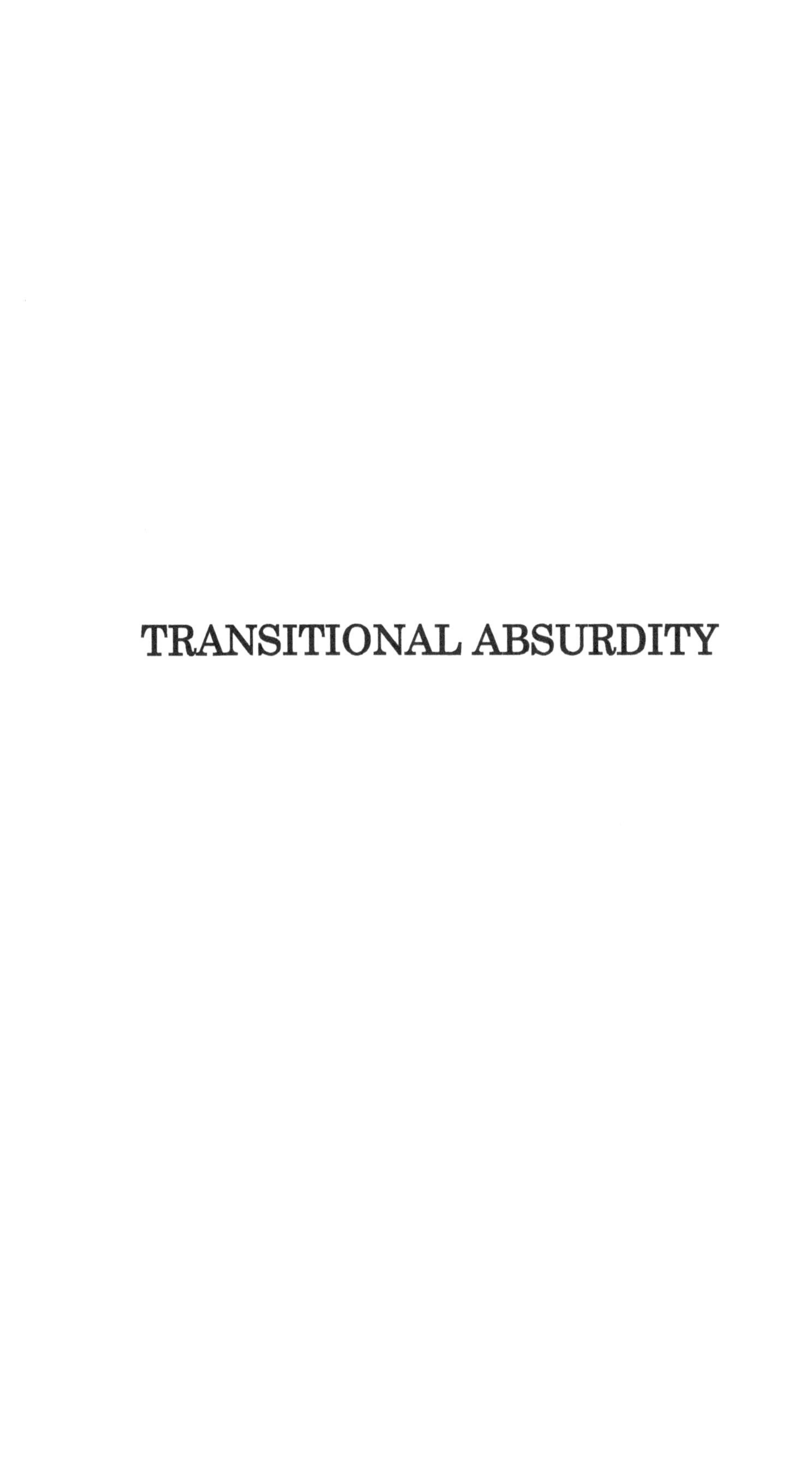

TRANSITIONAL ABSURDITY

Also by Charles Johnston:

The Creative Imperative: Human Growth and Planetary Evolution

Necessary Wisdom: Meeting the Challenge of a New Cultural Maturity

Pattern and Reality: A Brief Introduction to Creative Systems Theory
The Power of Diversity: An Introduction to the Creative Systems Personality Typology

An Evolutionary History of Music: Introducing Creative Systems Theory Through the Language of Sound (DVD)

Quick and Dirty Answers to the Biggest of Questions: Creative Systems Theory Explains What It Is All About (Really)

Cultural CMaturity: A Guidebook for the Future

Hope and the Future: Confronting Today's Crisis of Purpose

On the Evolution of Intimacy: A Brief Exploration into the Past, Present, and Future of Gender and Love

Rethinking How We Think: Integrative Meta-Perspective and the Cognitive "Growing Up" on Which Our Future Depends

Creative Systems Theory: A Comprehensive Theory of Purpose, Change, and Interrelationship in Human Systems (with Particular Pertinence to Un-Understanding the Times We Live in and the Tasks Ahead for the Species)

Perspective and Guidance for a Time of Deep Discord: Why We See Such Extreme Social and Political Polarization—and What We Can Do About It

Insight: Creative Systems Theory s Radical New Picture of Human Possibility

Intelligence's Creative Multiplicity: And Its Critical Role in the Future of Understanding

The Creative Systems Personality Typology: Engaging the Generative Roots of Diversity

Online:

Author/professional page: www.CharlesJohnstonMD.com

The Institute for Creative Development: www.CreativeSystems.org

The Creative Systems Personality Typology: www.CSPTHome.org

An Evolutionary History of Music: www.Evolmusic.org

Cultural Maturity: A Blog for the Future: www.CulturalMaturityBlog.net

Ask the Cultural Psychiatrist YouTube channel: youtube.com/@cjohnston

TRANSITIONAL ABSURDITY

A Reason for Hope / A Reason to Fear—Looking Squarely at the Future in Confusing and Contradictory Times

CHARLES M. JOHNSTON, MD

The Institute for Creative Development (ICD) Press

Seattle, Washington

Publisher's Cataloging-in-Publication
(Provided by Cassidy Cataloguing Services, Inc.).

Names: Johnston, Charles M., author.

Title: Transitional absurdity : a reason to hope/a reason to fear — looking squarely at the future in confusing and contradictory times / Charles M. Johnston, MD.

Description: Seattle, Washington : The Institute for Creative Development (ICD) Press, [2023] | Includes bibliographical references and index.

Identifiers: ISBN: 978-1-7342431-9-2 (paperback) | 979-8-9867952-1-8 (ebook) | LCCN: 2022924015

Subjects: LCSH: Typology (Psychology) | Temperament. | Personality. | Self-consciousness (Awareness) | Cultural pluralism--Psychological aspects | Social Evolution

Classification: LCC: HM626 .J64 2023 | DDC: 303.4--dc23

Cover design by Wilson Piechazek
Author photo by Brad Kelvin
Library of Congress Control Number: 2022924015
ISBN: 978-1-7342431-9-2
First Printing 2023

TRANSITIONAL ABSURDITY

INTRODUCTION

A Question That May Determine Our Future Well-Being

I don't know if the thesis of this book is correct. For a long time, the concept of Transitional Absurdity was not a topic I chose to write about, but today it seems essential that we take time to consider it. In our time, which easily seems not just confusing, but insane, Transitional Absurdity offers perspective that helps make this circumstance more understandable. But there is a more basic reason to take time with the concept: Unless the notion is accurate, I find it hard to be optimistic about our human future.

The lack of hope that permeates our world today is striking and troubling. As a psychiatrist who often works with young people, I find it particularly concerning. It is rare that someone I work with expresses optimism about what lies ahead. In fact, *I'm* not even sure that optimism is warranted. Our times confront us with multiple challenges of an existential sort—the possibility of nuclear annihilation, climate change and its potentially cataclysmic consequences, the ever-present dangers of global disease, and new information technologies that could run amok and be our undoing. Certainly times ahead will demand a great deal of humanity if we are to move forward in positive ways.

Along with being a psychiatrist, I'm also a futurist: I attempt to bring big-picture, long-term systemic perspective to the human condition. In contrast to most futurists who give greatest attention to technological advancement, the focus of my work is the human dimension. I'm interested in the ways we humans think and act have evolved—and continue to evolve in our time. This interest has taken primary expression in the development of Creative Systems

Theory, a comprehensive framework for understanding purpose, change, and interrelationship in human systems.[1] For many years I directed the Institute for Creative Development, a think tank and center for advanced leadership training in Seattle, Washington.[2]

I first coined the term Transitional Absurdity over forty years ago with the early development of the theory. At that time, I chose to exclude it from my writing for a couple of reasons, beyond the basic question of whether the concept is correct: I was concerned that the term would merely play into the thinking of people who use cynicism as a simple answer escape. (Such thinking is not only deadening; it is ultimately self-fulfilling.) And, at the time, things weren't going that badly. I felt that it made most sense to focus my writing on possibilities. And that, for the most part, is what I have done. Creative Systems Theory describes the potential for an important next chapter in the human story: a critical "growing up" as a species, which the theory calls Cultural Maturity. The concept of Cultural Maturity takes us forward and makes important new human capacities possible. And of particular pertinence to the question of hope, Creative Systems Theory describes how the potential for Cultural Maturity's changes is developmentally built into who we are. Over the years, I've written in detail about the new human capacities that Cultural Maturity's changes make possible, and how they should alter every part of our lives—from more personal concerns such as morality, identity, and love, to how we shape our institutions and make needed collective decisions.[3]

---

[1]   The theory is presented in most detailed form in my book Creative Systems Theory: A Comprehensive Theory of Purpose Change and Interrelationship in Human Systems, ICD Press, 2021.

[2]   See **www.creativesystems.org**

[3]   Besides my books, a couple of other resources prove particularly helpful in this regard. The Cultural Maturity Blog (**www.culturalmaturityblog.net**) addresses questions critical to our time from the perspective of Cultural Maturity. And the Ask the Cultural Psychiatrist YouTube channel (youtube.com/@cjohnstonmd) introduces how culturally mature understanding represents a needed "new common sense."

But the picture that the concept of Cultural Maturity presents is not all cheery. Cultural Maturity's changes are in no way guaranteed; possibility is not destiny. If we fail at what Cultural Maturity asks of us, we could very well be doomed. Furthermore, even if we make an honest effort toward needed changes, we will likely go through an awkward in-between time in the process of getting there. The theory simply calls this Transition. The concept of Transitional Absurdity describes some of the difficulties—and even ludicrousness—that we should expect in these transitional times.

Circumstances over the last thirty years have, for me, made the concept of Transitional Absurdity newly pertinent and worthy of addressing more explicitly. Numerous measures of human well-being have gone in the wrong direction—rates of anxiety, depression, obesity, addiction, suicide, gun violence, and life expectancy as a whole. Issues of every sort are increasingly becoming polarized and sources of antagonism. And we have witnessed dangerous backsliding with regard to many of the capacities that the concept of Cultural Maturity argues will be essential if we are to make good future choices.

Do transitional dynamics provide an explanation? Not for all of it. But if they do even in part, that provides important guidance. It also provides hope. It means that, while effectively advancing will stretch us in ways that we can only begin to imagine, there is at least a way forward, and it is way that is more than just possible. It would reward us both personally and collectively in profound ways.

This book is about such a possibility and the stretch that it will require. It is also about ways we may stumble and temporarily fall in confronting all that the transition may demand of us. Transitional Absurdities can have us thinking and acting in ways that are quite crazy. I write this book in the hope that we can learn from that craziness—that it might help us better understand the times in which we live and better appreciate what times ahead will require.

Chapter One briefly introduces the concept of Cultural Maturity and the dynamics of transition. It also addresses the reasons for predicting Transitional Absurdity and identifies some forms we expect such absurdity to take.

Chapters Two through Five each highlight one of those expected manifestations. They alert us to the traps that different kinds of Transitional Absurdities present and invite us to appreciate what getting beyond those traps will ask of us. Chapter Two looks at Transitional Absurdities that have their origins in denial and a failure to acknowledge the challenges that confront us. Chapter Three confronts Transitional Absurdities that are best understood as reactive responses to all that our time asks of us. Chapter Four addresses Transitional Absurdities that reflect "overshooting the mark," where ways of thinking and acting that have outlived their usefulness become exaggerated to extremes. And Chapter Five examines Transitional Absurdities that are products of misinterpreting today's postmodern challenges to historical truths in ways that leave us short of what the future ultimately requires.

Chapter Six turns more specifically to antidotes. It looks at ways we can use Transitional Absurdities as teachers instead of merely surrendering to the disorder and discomfort they create; and it reflects on possible consequences when we do. The book's Appendix provides basic introductions to Creative Systems Theory and the concept of Cultural Maturity. If you enjoy big-picture conceptual perspective you may find it of particular value, and even choose to start there; but most people will want to leave it to the end, particularly if you learn best by identifying challenges and concrete examples. In that case, the body of the book will provide sufficient conceptual background for your purposes.

CHAPTER ONE

Setting the Conceptual Stage

Making sense of the concept of Transitional Absurdity requires perspective of a more big-picture, long-term sort than we usually bring to concerns of a cultural type. News commentary rarely gets beyond the most recent electoral or business cycle, and academia is unlikely to question the basic assumptions of Modern Age thought. Proper understanding of the concept requires a perspective that spans centuries. It also requires that we entertain the possibility that what our times ask of us may be new, in a fundamental sense.

Here I will provide a closer look at the concept of Cultural Maturity and how it relates to the idea of Transitional Absurdity. I will then tie these reflections more specifically to current circumstances and explain why those circumstances are concerning. We will look briefly at how Creative Systems Theory provides conceptual context for these observations, examine what the theory calls the Dilemma of Trajectory, and explore the role that transitional dynamics play in the workings of developmental processes. Finally, we will focus on the mechanisms of Transitional Absurdity and the multiple ways those mechanisms manifest.

Cultural Maturity and Transitional Absurdity

In order to make sense of the concept of Transitional Absurdity, we need to employ Creative Systems Theory's concept of Cultural Maturity. It questions the widespread assumption that Modern Age belief systems and institutions represent a developmental ideal and end point; instead, the concept of Cultural Maturity proposes that we think of these cultural achievements as but one chapter in a larger story—and it goes on to describe a needed next chapter in that developmental story.

In my writings I've described how effectively addressing any of humanity's important challenges ahead will require new capacities. Cultural Maturity's changes make those new human capacities possible by bringing with it a new kind of responsibility in the human endeavor. It helps us get beyond the simple-minded, ideological beliefs of times past and to better tolerate—and creatively engage—uncertainty, complexity, and the fact of real limits. In addition, Cultural Maturity opens our eyes to the importance of systemic context—how the particulars that make something true depend on when and where we look.

While these new capacities are impressive, it is also the case that new cultural chapters rarely tend to arrive smoothly, and we expect disruption with Cultural Maturity's changes to be particularly pronounced. Given that any time of transition will be disruptive, in the sense of challenging familiar truth, transition between Modern Age realities and Cultural Maturity's more systemic perspectives alters experience in particularly fundamental ways. Most immediately it challenges culture's past mythologized significance. Historically we've related to culture as if it were a mythic parent; but the comforting absolutes of culture are ceasing to serve us in the same way. In contrast, Cultural Maturity requires that we understand with an encompassing completeness of perspective that has not before been an option. It requires not just letting go of familiar truths, but adopting a whole different relationship to truth.

Transitional Absurdity describes the craziness we might expect with this dramatic and fundamental kind of disruption. Another Creative System Theory notion—the concept of Capacitance—lets us be more specific. When any system faces challenges that are greater than it can readily tolerate, it may respond with denial or regression. Or it may polarize, with the black-or-white world that results, effectively keeping the challenge to Capacitance at a safe arm's length. It may also protect itself from the full implications of what is being asked by stalling partway through the change process, leaving essential aspects of the challenge unaddressed.

The Last Thirty Years

How much of what we find confusing and contradictory in our time can we understand in terms of Transitional dynamics, and more specifically in terms of Transitional Absurdity? I don't know any more important question when it comes to making sense of the times we live in and discerning whether there is reason to be optimistic about the future.

Certainly, today we see many positive aspects of Culture Maturity's predictions. Over the last century, we have witnessed important challenges to traditional truths; and we have seen the beginnings of new ways of thinking in several fields, increasing possibilities and gradually revealing a more nuanced and systemically complex world.

But, particularly over the last thirty years, we've also witnessed behavior that we are hard-pressed to describe in any way as sane. I've written extensively about key examples. Undoubtedly, we are seeing a deterioration of our general collective mental health. Previously I noted a general decline of hope and a growing prevalence of several conditions that are often called afflictions of despair—depression, addiction, suicide, and gun violence. Creative Systems Theory talks of a modern Crisis of Purpose. The last thirty years have seen a rise of nearly all indicators of such a crisis.

Related is the denial of critical issues like climate change and increasing species extinction. Such issues could result in great pain if not dealt with wisely. And while the warning signs might have been impossible to ignore, efforts over the last thirty years have failed to meet the challenge.

I've given particular attention in my writing to today's growing social and political polarization. Today we encounter polarization around issues of every sort, with people dividing almost immediately into opposite camps. Such knee-jerk polarization pits neighbor against neighbor and directly undermines the making of effective decisions. People have always had differences; but this kind of reactive, absolutist polarization is new, and it is a major concern if we are to get along and have any kind of effective governance.

We've also seen more explicitly regressive dynamics around the globe. Decades ago, the fall of the Berlin Wall and what people called an "Arab Spring" promised important steps forward on the global stage. Today, with increasing frequency, we witness failures of fledgling attempts at democratic rule and growing authoritarian tendencies in even advanced nations.

We can also identify backsliding in specialized cultural spheres. A colleague of mine who is a Catholic nun recently shared her disappointment that the ecumenical conferences common in the last decades of the previous century (which brought together people from far-flung faiths) have become rare. I've witnessed something similar in my own field. I remember a national gathering organized by psychiatrist Milton Ericsson in 1988 that invited the best thinkers from each of the often-warring schools of psychological thought to join in conversation. I've not experienced anything of such depth since. Late in the 20th century, books and newsletters that articulated post-partisan political perspective were also common. These observations not only provide further evidence of regression; they also follow the timeline that I have suggested.

I find a more recent phenomenon especially worrying—that of our relationship with new technologies. Our devices increasingly co-opt our attention by seducing us with pseudo-significance and introducing addictive dynamics. But while seductive distractions are hardly new, and emerging digital technologies can serve us in many ways, it is the pervasiveness of this influence that is new and presents real dangers. Add the powers of artificial intelligence and inevitably we get the invention of ever more powerful digital designer drugs. These dangers are increasingly being recognized. But the fact that we have not taken them more seriously is a particularly consequential kind of contemporary blindness that could well be our undoing.

Why We See What We Do

Transitional Absurdity is only one explanation for the denial, backsliding, and often simple blindness that we have witnessed in recent times. In my writing, I've suggested other legitimate reasons, each with different implications for the ways in which we should respond.

It is possible that today's challenges are proving simply too much for us, and if this circumstance continues, the future will not be bright. Indeed, if nothing else intervenes to alter where we are headed, in the long term we may in fact be doomed. There would really be nothing we could do.

It is also possible that what we confront reflects the typical two-step-forward-one-step-back way of societal change. We could merely be going through a rough patch that calls for greater responsibility and commitment, but nothing fundamentally new. Many respected thinkers today are reminding us that we can have democracy only if we are willing to defend it. Such counsel is wholly consistent with a traditional view that makes government as we have known it an ideal and an end point. If that is the case, great concern is not warranted.

Transition Absurdity represents a third kind of possibility. While more radical, of the interpretations I have noted I find it most consistent with what we see. And given that it is most consistent with a vital human future, I cross my fingers that it is the correct one. We find evidence for it in the fact that many of the realities that threaten to overwhelm us in our time are products of the realities that Cultural Maturity's changes make possible. Much in what we see may reflect the kind of awkward, in-between dynamics that systems manifest as they struggle to engage major changes. And being that Cultural Maturity's changes are of a particularly encompassing and transformative sort, we would expect such dynamics to be comparably pronounced. It is not unreasonable to think that much in the troubling realities of the last thirty years might be a response to being stretched in ways that, at least initially, are confusing and disorienting.

Cultural Maturity's changes will ask a lot of us. But if today's craziness is best thought of as a reflection of an awkward in-between time in its realization, there is legitimate reason for hope. And with a little understanding, the concepts of Transitional Absurdity and Cultural Maturity provide essential guidance in taking necessary steps forward.

The Evolution of Narrative

Taking a moment to reflect more specifically on narrative and its current evolution helps put this picture in larger perspective. People's conclusions about the tasks of our time tend to fall into a few basic categories. Some see the modern challenge primarily in terms of refining what we have known. Creative Systems Theory calls this a "We've Arrived" narrative. Such narratives assume that current ways of thinking and current institutional forms reflect a kind of ideal, an end point in culture's story.

It is important to appreciate how powerfully this Modern Age narrative has served us. It effectively took us beyond the absolutist hierarchies and religious orthodoxies of medieval times. But in our time, it is equally important that we recognize that it isn't sufficient going forward, as evidenced by today's Crisis of Purpose. Our Modern Age story no longer creates meaning in our lives in the same way as in times past. Also, in more conceptual ways the Modern Age narrative today fails to hold up; its story remains materialistic, rationalistic, and individualistic. And it has expressed itself in cleanly-cleaved, polar juxtapositions such as masculine versus feminine, fact versus feelings, and us versus them. The concept of Cultural Maturity describes our need for ways of thinking that better reflect all that matters to us, the full complexity of how we understand, and who we are—not just as individuals, but as members of a larger shared experience.

A couple of other common narratives, seemingly opposite to one another, also fail us by providing little of real value. Utopian narratives promise some ultimate kind of realization, either technological or spiritual. Dystopian narratives assume that in some fundamental way we have failed. The important recognition is that, in the end, each can get in the way of needed understanding. Dystopian views, besides blinding us to possibilities, easily become self-fulfilling prophecies. And utopian narratives, in the end just the other side of the coin to their dystopian cousins, provide safe illusions that distort the magnitude of what our times actually ask of us.

In recent decades, we've also witnessed more postmodern narratives. The postmodernist appreciates that the cultural absolutes of times past no longer provide the benefit they once did. And from a culturally mature perspective, postmodern conclusions recognize a newly multifaceted and often uncertain reality in which meaning is increasingly ours to determine. But postmodern thought gets us only partway; it fails in the most consequential piece of the task: While it recognizes the limitations of the past's absolutist ideological beliefs, it is capable only of beginning to grasp what, if anything, might lie beyond them. Except in the best of formulations, it easily reduces to an "anything goes," "different-strokes-for-different-folks" reality in which one truth is as good as another. Arbitrariness gets confused with significance. Later I will devote a whole chapter to this kind of Transitional Absurdity.

Transitional Absurdities are the products of these variously limited—and limiting—kinds of stories and the suggestion that anything of significance might exist beyond them. Whether modernist, dystopian, utopian, or postmodernist, these familiar narratives fail to provide anything that can heal today's Crisis of Purpose. They also fail to supply the capacities needed to move forward. For me, the most compelling argument for the concept of Cultural Maturity is that it offers a new guiding narrative, a "North Star" for our actions that is consistent not only with effective decision-making, but also with a desirable future existence.

Creative Systems Theory and Cultural Maturity

To fully understand either Cultural Maturity or the concept of Transitional Absurdity, we need to view these notions in the larger context of Creative Systems Theory (CST). Creative Systems Theory takes as its conceptual starting point the question of what most defines us as humans. Some have suggested that it is our use of language; others, our capacities for conceptual abstraction or complex social relationships. But Creative Systems Theory argues that another attribute underlies each of these abilities: our robust capacity to create. We are "toolmakers," and creators not just of things but also of ideas and social structures; and, of particular pertinence to our tasks here, makers of meaning.

Creative Systems Theory addresses how human systems of all sorts—individuals, families, communities, institutions, and cultures—grow and interrelate. To this end, the theory provides a big-picture perspective for understanding why we humans believe the often odd and contradictory things we do, including the evolution of thoughts we consider to be true, whether in our personal lives, in relationships, or at different stages in a culture's story. CST also explains why we see our worlds as we do at particular points in time.

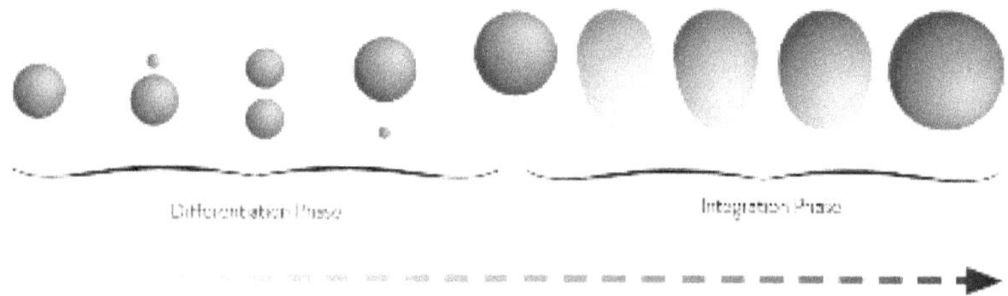

Fig. 1-1. The Creative Function

The Creative Function, conceived by Creative Systems Theory and illustrated in Figure 1-1, maps the formative process for creations of all sorts.

The first half of any creative formative process involves creative differentiation. The new creation first buds off from its original context. It then grows and evolves, with each stage becoming more developed and more separate from its creative context. The second half of the process brings more specifically integrative dynamics, where we speak of the new and radical as having become "second nature." In an individual's lifetime, we may see more integrative processes that invite the possibility of becoming not just more intelligent, but wise.

The Creative Function helps us make sense of the concept of Cultural Maturity. This concept has to do with second-half mechanisms as they manifest in culture as creative processes. Cultural Maturity involves a couple of key change dynamics. First, we stop relating to culture as a mythic parent. In times past, cultural truths typically have been mythologized, seen almost as God-given. Cultural Maturity challenges us to take a new, more complete kind of responsibility for the choices we make in our individual and collective lives.

Second, we confront the integrative mechanisms inherent to maturity in any creative/formative process. In doing so, Cultural Maturity brings forth the ability to more deeply engage the whole of our cognitive complexity. The result is called Integrative Meta-perspective. While the term is a bit of a mouthful, it describes the dynamic quite precisely. To help clarify what is involved, I often use the image of a box of crayons. Integrative Meta-perspective enables us to step back and consciously draw on the whole box in a way not before possible.

We recognize this kind of integrative mechanism in individual psychological development, as our later years can bring with them the ability to "bridge" polar opposites—key to the possibility of greater wisdom. We find an increased ability to get our minds around what before seemed only like either/ors—such as good versus evil and certainty versus uncertainty. The concept of Cultural Maturity proposes that we are now seeing the beginnings of something parallel in the developmental dynamics of culture.

The Dilemma of Trajectory

The Dilemma of Trajectory refers to a quandary inherent to the mid-point of any formative process. A good way to think about it draws on language from psychology and myth. Polarities are not merely opposites: They reflect a predictable kind of symmetry, juxtaposing qualities that are more archetypal masculine (harder and more manifest) with qualities that are more archetypal feminine (softer and more receptive).

Creative Systems Theory describes how we see a progression over the first half of any creative/formative process from realities where the archetypally feminine has the greater influence to realities in which the archetypally masculine is most dominant. Note that, with transition (the mid-point in any developmental process), this trajectory of change brings us to what might appear to be a dead end, where only the archetypally masculine remains. There can seem nowhere further to go. Creative Systems Theory calls this the Dilemma of Trajectory.

Framing the Dilemma of Trajectory in terms of the evolution of difference helps make its implications more concrete. Each stage in any developmental process's first half produces greater emphasis on difference—distance between polar extremes and difference more generally. At Transition, this defining impetus reaches an extreme. The Dilemma of Trajectory brings attention to how going further in this direction really stops being an option (Figure 1-2).

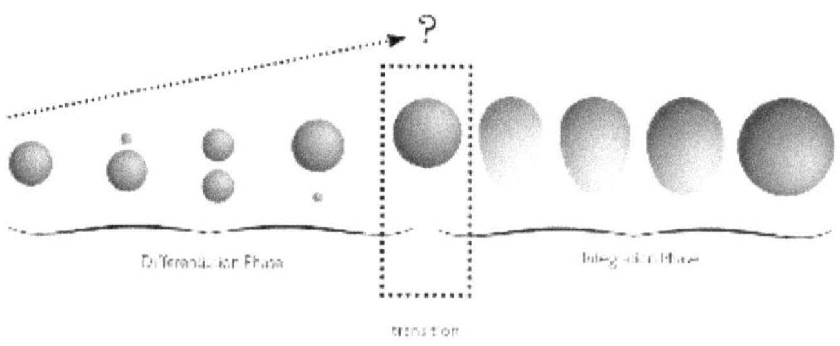

Fig. 1-2. The Dilemma of Trajectory

We see this with personal development. The first half of personal psychological development is marked by processes that produce ever-greater independence, individuality, and authority over the world around us—each an expression of increasing separation and emphasis on difference. This general direction of change in effect defines growth in the first half of our lives. But in an individual life's second half, it stops serving us in the same way. Indeed, if we continue as we have, the second half of life becomes increasingly absurd, at best a thin caricature of youth.

In a similar way, history to this point has produced ever-greater emphasis on distinction. Each cultural stage has brought a growing impetus toward independence and individual authority, from the early rise of civilization's separation from nature; to later, the Magna Carta's affirmation of basic human privilege and the Declaration of Independence proclamation of the individual's right to the pursuit of happiness. History has also brought ever-greater perceived control over the world around us, culminating with the Industrial Age promising an ultimate kind of human dominion, and today's Information Age giving that promise all-encompassing expression.

While such achievement could not have been more significant, as was Transition in individual development, this developmental trajectory has stopped serving us. Although much of what we have reaped and will continue to reap is owing to our individuality and autonomy of choice; the future equally cries out for a new appreciation of our relatedness, a fresh understanding of caring, community, and the common good. And while culture's evolution has also brought with it increasing human control—over nature, over our bodies, over life's deep mysteries—today what is needed is a new humility to what we *cannot* control, a new emphasis on listening rather than directing, whether the voice needing attention is the natural world, our tissues, or the unfathomable.

We can usefully frame the Dilemma of Trajectory in terms of leadership, which is what Cultural Maturity is ultimately about. Today we confront profound questions; indeed, questions with God-like implications. But the authority needed to address them is not some ascension to a chair of final dominion (we somehow becoming God). Neither is it some further iteration of the Enlightenment's grand goal of bringing all understanding into the pure light of awareness and realizing control over the untamed. Surely, many of the problems we face in today's world derive from just such hubristic notions of what "right action" is about. We are left in a pickle that cannot be resolved by continuing on the course we have known. If more systemic understanding is in fact what today's new questions require, then culturally mature perspective—or at least something that provides a similar, more aware and integrative outcome—becomes the only real option.

Framing the Dilemma of Trajectory in creative terms brings attention to the fundamental nature of these consequences and the depths of their implications. At Transition we stand in a world of all content and no context, of all right hand and no left, of life as ultimate abstraction stretched ever more distant from experience's roots. Taken far enough, proceeding further in this direction of distinction and separation leads to circumstances that are not only ludicrous, but ultimately self-destructive. Continuing in this way threatens to sever us from much that is most important in being human—such as the body, the child's world of imagination, our human connectedness with one another, and our felt relationship with the spiritual and with nature.

Transitional Absurdity

Transitional Absurdities are protective mechanisms that occur in response to the startling realities we find with Transition and the considerable demands of Cultural Maturity. Applying the concept of Transitional Absurdity requires care. As with other tools of critique, it can become a repository for any phenomenon that our particular world view finds aversive. Only when we understand it as a very specific concept requiring very particular discernments, it provides important insight and perspective.

The protective mechanisms that comprise Transitional Absurdities can be placed into four basic groups. Some Transitional Absurdities protect us by helping us ignore, or "stop short," of what is being asked of us. By using simple denial as their most common form, they function to keep Cultural Maturity's demands at a safe distance. Another group of Transitional Absurdities are protective reactions to feeling overwhelmed by the sheer magnitude of current challenges. Today's extreme polarization in the social and political spheres may exemplify this type of "regressive" Transitional Absurdity. Still others "overshoot the mark." They apply outmoded, onward-and-upward ways of thinking to questions that now demand much more of us. Additional Transitional Absurdities, which we call "postmodern," misinterpret today's loss of past cultural absolutes. These confuse anything-goes Transitional realities with the deeper understanding on which our future depends.

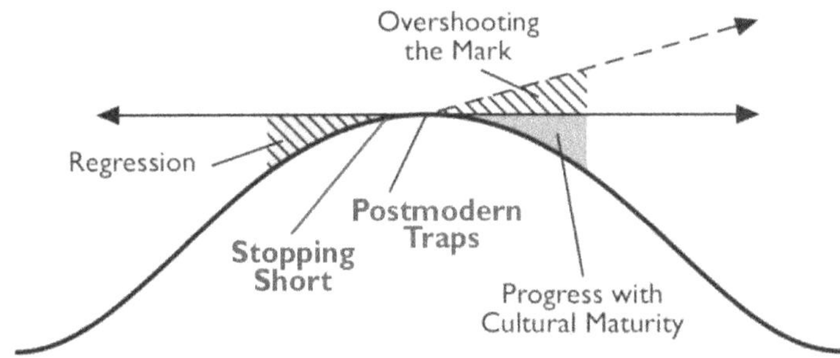

Fig. 1-3. Transitional Absurdity and the Dilemma of Trajectory

These four kinds of Transitional Absurdity (Figure 1-3) will provide the structure for the book's next four chapters. Taking a moment for a few additional words about each of them provides a foundation for the book's more detailed reflections.

The first and most easily grasped type of Transitional Absurdity involves simply keeping Cultural Maturity's demands at arm's length. We see it with today's Crisis of Purpose. Not only do we lack a story adequate for our time, but we fail to recognize that this is the case. This "stopping-short" Transitional

Absurdity is also apparent when we fail to appreciate the need for culturally mature capacities, such as respecting the environmental limits necessary to reverse global warming and species extinction. Similarly, we've commonly ignored economic limits by failing to appreciate the dangers inherent in extreme income inequality, and the need to fundamentally rethink wealth and progress.

The second kind of Transitional Absurdity is not so much a product of missing the big picture as it is of reacting in less-than-helpful ways to its demands. I think of current partisan insanity as reactive in this sense. Extreme polarization is a common response when systems are challenged past levels they can handle. We see such reactive dynamics in the kind of social regression taking place on the planet, with the growing prevalence of authoritarian leadership that promises order and stability in the context of today's easily overwhelming uncertainties and complexities.

Many of the most consequential Transitional Absurdities represent the third group, overshooting the mark, in the transition from Modern Age realities into Cultural Maturity's needed next cultural chapter. When we overshoot the mark, mechanisms that have served us in the past become amplified and distorted. Overshooting the mark conclusions manifest in particularly consequential ways with techno-utopian beliefs that promise an almost spiritual kind of salvation and blind us to essential complexities. But they also take more everyday expression in the common assumption that current institutions and ways of thinking—governmental, economic, educational, scientific—represent some last word.

The final kind of Transitional Absurdity finds us, in effect, stuck halfway. We can think of it in relation to what I've referred to as postmodern belief. With this mechanism, traditional cultural absolutes of times past get replaced not by more systemic understanding, but by beliefs that make one choice as good as any other. Truth becomes arbitrary, a function of little more than whim; and identity becomes pretty much anything we might choose. Such postmodern arbitrariness leads to "fake news" and "alternative facts." I will give particular attention to how this halfway kind of result manifests with modern identity politics. While current conversations about gender, race, and identity are making important contributions, often they result in ideological conclusions that become obstacles to the needed outcome. We will also examine how moral questions require us to think in new ways and how Cultural Maturity challenges us to bring a new sophistication to our understanding of history.

How the Concept of Transitional Absurdity Helps Us

Most immediately, the concept of Transitional Absurdity alerts us to the fact that much that we take for granted in our time is not at all sane. That is, the concept focuses attention on behaviors that are inconsistent with our ultimate human well-being.

The concept of Transitional Absurdity helps us make better sense of what we see. We may not celebrate what the concept alerts us to, but at the least it helps us avoid responding to unpleasant circumstances in reactive ways that could make realities worse. The concept describes how circumstances that might seem quite crazy—indeed that might seem only to promise the end of us—can be predicted. If we understand the dynamics that create those circumstances, we can appreciate them as consequences of larger processes that potentially take us forward.

In addition, by highlighting the importance of culturally mature capacities, Transitional Absurdity brings attention to what is needed if we are to effectively advance. If the concept of Cultural Maturity is correct, it is these new capacities that must provide the needed stability and sanity as we engage in the essential challenges before us. I've often referred to Cultural Maturity as a needed "new common sense." The concept of Transitional Absurdity helps make clear how Cultural Maturity may be the only game in town as we look to the future.

In the decades immediately before us, we will likely see inspiring examples of culturally mature leadership and much in the way of good and wise decision-making that will move us deeply. And certainly we will also encounter absurdities, instabilities, and even cataclysms, some of which may try us mightily. The concept of Transitional Absurdity can help us find the courage and commitment to confront potentially overwhelming realities and to take on Cultural Maturity's essential demands.

CHAPTER TWO

Transitional Absurdity and Our Modern Crisis of Purpose

Our first kind of Transitional Absurdity involves stopping short of Transition's demands, or at least barely beginning to make our way in relationship to them. I think of today's Crisis of Purpose in this way. This is also how I interpret the fact that afflictions of despair have come to define our time. In addition, I will highlight those ways of stopping short that reveal the absence of essential, culturally mature capacities, such as a required new maturity in our relationship with limits, if we are to address severe environmental challenges. I will also address how the absence of meaning in people's lives is easily co-opted. And I will end by examining what it might mean to address collective purpose more consciously and systemically.

Confronting Our Time's Crisis of Purpose

I introduced my short book *Hope and the Future* by describing a young man I had seen in therapy who had attempted to hang himself. As our work progressed, it became strikingly clear that the hopelessness he felt was personal only in limited ways; it had more to do with realities in the larger world. He described having a hard time thinking of a future that he would want to be a part of.

I gave that book the subtitle, "Confronting Today's Crisis of Purpose" and made the notion of a modern Crisis of Purpose a formal concept within Creative Systems Theory. A good way to think about today's Crisis of Purpose is that it is a crisis of narrative. The guiding stories we have known and lived by—the American Dream, progress's promise of ever onward-and-upward advancement, opposing political ideologies, the beliefs of our various religious traditions—have stopped serving us in the same ways. Without a cultural story that is coherent and compelling, it is hard to have hope.

The recognition that familiar cultural stories are no longer working provides a starting place for understanding today's Crisis of Purpose. But we need more if we are to make sense of the lack of optimism so many people feel today. If the concept of Transitional Absurdity is correct, a loss of the narrative we have known is not all that is involved. Transitional dynamics make what we see more understandable and add important nuance.

I've touched on the big pieces. There is the way Cultural Maturity's cognitive changes require that we surrender what in times past has been in effect a parent/child relationship with culture. It is not just that we are losing familiar narratives; we are challenged to give up what has made past narratives powerful and directly tied to meaning. We've always mythologized our cultural stories: in identification with nation and place, with religious doctrine, or simply with the assumption that our particular cultural mores represented some final truth. But as culture's parental authority falls away, we become responsible for the truths we draw on. We also necessarily step forward into a more complex and uncertainty-permeated world, one in which all reassuring absolutes no longer apply.

These circumstances would be demanding enough without the Dilemma of Trajectory. I've described how Transitional dynamics distance us from essential aspects of that which makes us human—any depth of connection with bodily experience, nature, our receptivity, and with others in community. Just as we are having to take new responsibility for questions of truth and purpose in our lives, we find ourselves losing touch with much that is most needed to effectively take on the task.

And that is not all. We also face the fact that successfully taking on the challenges ahead requires the new kinds of capacities that Cultural Maturity's changes make possible. I've noted the importance of better tolerating uncertainty, complexity, and the fact of real limits. I've also mentioned the ability to better appreciate systemic context. As we first approach Cultural Maturity's threshold, these new capacities are not yet available to us. But they will be needed if we are to effectively address all kinds of personal challenges going forward—from those of identity to requirements for love and moral discernment. They will also be needed if we are to effectively address challenges that we must confront together, such as the risks of nuclear proliferation, climate change, pandemics, and the often two-edged implications of technological advancements. Without new capacities, we can easily feel that answers simply don't exist and that there is no place to hide.

Faced with a lack of direction for our lives and dynamics that stretch us in fundamental ways, it is not surprising that we might often in our time feel rudderless and overwhelmed. One way we have protected ourselves is with denial, by stopping short and failing to look squarely at our challenges. As developments in recent decades have made these new realities increasingly inescapable, it is reasonable that we could respond in ways that might seem absurd—and often simply are.

Afflictions of Despair

I've tied the concept of Transitional Absurdity to today's growing prevalence of "afflictions of despair." The connection with depression, addiction, and suicide is most obvious. It should not surprise us that people might respond to the lack of guiding story with despondency, or in ways that offer escape, whether momentary, as with addiction; or permanently. People today often talk more specifically of "diseases and deaths of despair," such as our increasing rates of chronic afflictions such as diabetes, heart disease, and the obesity epidemic. Using the general concept of Transitional Absurdity in an even more systemically encompassing way, I include psychological dynamics, such as the lack of basic civility while relating to one another, or the increasing rates of gun violence.

Particularly disturbing is the despair felt by our young people. A recent report from the U.S. Centers for Disease Control and Prevention (CDC) reported that 42 percent of U.S. high schoolers experienced persistent feelings of sadness or hopelessness in 2021, while 22 percent seriously considered suicide. And an analysis of 4,767,840 pediatric hospitalizations by researchers at Dartmouth, published in the *Journal of the American Medical Association* (*JAMA*), found that between 2009 and 2019 mental health hospitalization increased by 25.8 percent. Especially striking is the rise of suicidal behavior. The percentage of pediatric mental health hospitalizations involving suicidal or self-hating behavior rose to 64.2 percent in 2019 from 30.7 percent in 2009. General death rates among America's youth increased by 10.7 percent from 2019 to 2020, and 8.3 percent from 2020 to 2021. Guns were responsible for almost half of the increase from 2019 to 2020 as homicides among children aged ten to nineteen grew by 39 percent.

Afflictions of despair are certainly not limited to our young people. Suicide rates in general have increased in recent decades, particularly for men in their middle years. Neither are these afflictions limited to those we think of in psychological terms. In the United States in recent years we have seen a decrease in general life expectancy, something that we have not witnessed in a century. Some of this is explained by ever more dangerous opioids such as fentanyl, and increasing rates of gun violence. But neither of these explain all of it. We are also seeing increasing rates of chronic illnesses and what seems a general diminishing of resilience.

We are left with important questions. First, is it legitimate to lump together phenomena as different as depression, addiction, chronic diseases, and gun violence? Historically, we have tended to think of them separately and assume they have separate solutions; but combining them seems to me appropriate if for no other reason than the fact that we have seen similar increases in each of these adversities over recent decades. Also, each of them has proven similarly impervious to intervention, in spite of our best efforts.

We also need to ask whether it makes sense to think of all these phenomena as reflections of Transitional Absurdity. At the least, each is understandable as a response to the stressors and common craziness of today's world. And the simple fact that people use terms like "diseases of despair" and "deaths of despair" suggests that at some level we recognize that what is going on is somehow tied to hope and purpose. I find this conclusion worth considering because it provides both an explanation consistent with the evidence and a pointer to viable antidotes.

A Closer Look

A closer look at two examples where the connection might not seem obvious—the opioid crisis and increasing rates of gun violence—helps paint the larger picture. Each example reflects a broad societal scourge whose incidences have increased dramatically over the last thirty years. With both, common explanations are at best partial, and proposed solutions have proven insufficient. And each ties in a particularly direct way to what we might expect to see with a felt lack of story and purpose.

It is hard to underestimate the amount of damage the opioid epidemic has caused, especially with the appearance of increasingly powerful and deadly synthetic opioids. In the county where I live, fentanyl was responsible for over 700 fatal overdoses last year, roughly triple the death toll of traffic accidents and gun violence combined. I've worked with two firefighters who were also emergency medical technicians (EMTs) in the last few years who decided to quit their professions (which they otherwise loved) because of the stress of dealing with the fentanyl epidemic. More than half of their calls were for fentanyl overdoses, and all too often there was little they could do.

To understand how the opioid crisis might relate to Transitional Absurdity, we need to reflect briefly on the mechanisms of addiction. Addictive substances all work in the same way: by creating artificial substitutes for real meaning. Depending on the drug, the kind of meaning may be different, and who will be most attracted to it will also be different: but the mechanism is the same. Opioids in particular create a sense of euphoria, and they effectively insulate us from the pain of daily life.

The relationship between addiction and purpose is confirmed by a necessary ingredient in any effective addiction treatment. When I work with someone suffering from addiction of any sort, I always start by asking where the person finds meaning in their life. If they have a hard time answering my question, we explore how real meaning might be found. Addiction can be very hard to beat, particularly opioid addiction. But when intervention *is* successful, it is because a person has begun to realize that authentic felt purpose is sacred. They stop being willing to accept artificial substitutes.

Over recent decades we've seen increased rates of addiction not just to opioids, but to alcohol, to food, and to our electronic devices. The social sciences have plenty of explanations, but they are not sufficiently encompassing to explain what they see. And interventions are rarely more than a band-aid. The time frame in which we have seen these increases supports the idea that we might think of today's addiction epidemic as a prime example of stop short Transitional Absurdity.

Today's epidemic of gun violence is similarly horrendous. According to the latest data from the CDC, 48,830 people died from gun-related injuries in the U.S. during 2021. That is nearly an 8 percent increase from 2020, which itself was a record-breaking year. Between 2016 and 2021, the number of deaths from gun violence increased by 6,000, or almost 40 percent. The number of teens killed or injured by guns was up 47 percent, and the number of children injured by guns was up 60 percent. While more than half the total in 2021 were suicides, the number of mass shootings has also gone up significantly of late, according to figures from the Gun Violence Archive, a non-profit research database. In each of the last three years there have been more than 600—almost two per day—on average. Such numbers become particularly chilling when the targets are schools and young children, as is so often the case today.

As with addiction, common attempts to explain the rise in gun violence tend to fail. And antidotes suggested by both the Left and the Right tend to inflame political debate rather than provide solutions. Offering few answers that would really make a difference, each side only doubles down on its limited conclusions in response to the ever-increasing carnage. However, the debate offers insight that helps us put this concerning picture more in the context of Transitional Absurdity. The Left names the availability of guns as the problem, and I support most proposals that would make it harder to obtain guns, particularly legislation that limits availability of assault rifles and the like, which have no justifiable place in a sane society. Also, the data shows that gun control can make a difference. But I have no illusions that such proposals would eliminate the problem. If those intent on doing harm really want a gun, they will find a way to get it. As a psychiatrist, however, I see one way that gun control efforts could make a big difference—by reducing suicide. When guns are not in people's everyday proximity, they are much less likely to be used impulsively in moments of despondency. But when any kind of planning is involved, even the most stringent of restrictions can have at best a limited effect.

The Right takes the position that it is the people committing the acts that are the problem. In response to recent events, this side proposes either red-flag laws that attempt to identify those who might commit such acts; or beefing up security in schools by their design or through a more direct law enforcement presence. Red-flag laws similarly have a place. But as mental health professionals know, identifying and stopping people whose instability make them vulnerable to committing such acts is extremely difficult because the majority of people who commit such crimes have no obvious psychiatric symptoms. The idea of protecting our schools—ensuring that they are physically secured and that school personnel are trained in protective procedures—also has value. But turning schools into fortresses is the last thing we need when kids already feel unsafe (and too often already feel that school is like prison).

Transitional Absurdity and today's Crisis of Purpose provides a more encompassing explanation of today's gun violence epidemic. It begins to make sense when we recognize that shootings are not alone in the phenomena they represent. Our time's increasing prevalence of gun-mediated violent acts can be understood as a reflection of the general desperation, anger, and hopelessness increasingly prevalent in society.

Importantly, if this interpretation is correct, we also find in it the possibility of solutions. When we bring culturally mature perspective to bear with gun violence, at the least we find ourselves more aware of when we reward and romanticize violence, and much less willing to tolerate such self-destructiveness. We also become less satisfied with polarized explanations. Of particular importance, Cultural Maturity's changes—by providing a new kind of guiding story—work as a direct antidote to feelings of estrangement and alienation. Specifically with regard to gun violence, by helping to better connect us with real significance in our lives, they make pseudo-significance of all kinds, including that provided by violent acts, much less attractive.

Denial in the Face of Essential Challenges

Transitional Absurdity of the stopping-short type is especially obvious with environmental concerns such as climate change and species extinction. These concerns warrant special attention in part because they relate so directly to people's feelings of hopelessness. Stopping short of what is needed to address these issues over recent decades has been particularly affecting, especially for our young people. But they also further the crisis we face not just with regard to what we think, but *how* we think. Effectively addressing today's profound environmental challenges will require capacities that become fully available to us only with Cultural Maturity's growing up as a species. That includes not only the basic ability to take greater responsibility; but also capacities needed for effective foresight, such as greater acceptance of uncertainty and complexity, and especially the fact of real limits.

Climate change will impact us profoundly, and it is already doing so. Most immediately, we see its effects on temperatures, which are rising to ever more unhealthy levels. We will also see more drought, extreme weather events, flooding, sea level rise, displacement of populations, greater prevalence of disease, and famine. Any one of these circumstances by itself could result in immense harm; and, combined with other challenges, could create even more dangerous realities. One of the greatest risks of climate change is that the disruptions that come with warming temperatures will increase conflict on the planet and the likelihood of deploying weapons of mass destruction.

We have in fact made significant progress of late in addressing the climate change crisis, particularly in the development of clean energy; but we can't forget how long it has taken us to get there. In 1988, Dr. James E. Hansen of the National Aeronautics and Space Administration (NASA) told a Congressional subcommittee that it was 99 percent certain that the warming trend we have seen over the last century is not a natural variation, but is caused by a buildup of carbon dioxide and other artificial gases in the atmosphere. And he was only one of many voices speaking out strongly at that time.

Over three decades ago, I wrote an article in which I made the argument that the climate change debate was in effect over. I based this conclusion not on a belief that we had somehow answered the question of whether man-made global warming was real, but rather on the fact that this was the wrong question. Whether we should take climate change seriously hinges not on whether we can be certain about the science (which we never can be, absolutely, by the nature of science); but on basic systemic risk assessment. I proposed that by that measure there was really nothing to debate.

I used the metaphor of Russian roulette to make my point: Say a person makes the accurate, limits-related observation that we can't know with absolute certainty that global climate change is real, then uses the observation to justify failing to respond to the threat. I will first ask the person what they think the odds are that human-caused climate change is in fact under way and could have dangerous consequences. I make them commit to a number. I then ask how they feel about their children playing Russian roulette. Few people are willing to claim that the odds of global warming being real and significant are lower than Russian roulette's one in six. And of the few who might, most will have a hard time escaping the recognition that their conclusion has more to do with ideology than carefully considered evaluation.

In fact, the science suggests we are playing with at least five bullets in the gun's cylinder, not only one. And even if there were just one, that would be far from a sane circumstance. Indeed, it is not being overly dramatic—simply observing what most anyone would consider obvious were the gun held by an individual rather than a species—to say it is suicidal. The origin of this suicidal circumstance is not any desire to do harm; rather it is simply denial, stopping short of being willing to look at the obvious. But this fact makes the reality no less consequential—or any more sane.

The best estimate of a temperature increase we could tolerate without major disruption is 1.5 degrees centigrade. However, even if we succeed with current efforts to curb global warming, we likely will see a rise of between 2.0 and 2.5 degrees centigrade regardless. But that is far less damaging than the four or five degrees rise that we would likely witness if we took no steps. It is a level that countries in the Global North can likely endure, albeit with significant consequences. It will be much harder for nations in the Global South, where, between 2030 and 2050, climate change is expected to cause approximately 250,000 additional deaths per year from malnutrition, malaria, diarrhea, and heat stress.

Culturally mature perspective alerts us to the way that effectively addressing climate change will ask of us something deeper than merely being smarter or more informed. We can make a start by opening our eyes to the obvious; but acting proactively with needed nuance and complexity will require new steps in how we understand—and, in an important sense, in being who we are. Ultimately it will require a new kind of cultural narrative—one that makes the need for a newly grown-up sense of responsibility and foresight obvious. It will also require more specific capacities new to us as a species, and in particular a new maturity in our relationship to limits.

In important ways, species extinction represents an even more fundamental contemporary failure. It is a kind of stopping short that we expect to particularly impact our young people. Here we've barely made a beginning either in terms of sufficiently acknowledging what is at stake or in devising solutions. Again, the challenge is a whole new cultural story, one that puts forward the need for accepting responsibility, effective foresight, and acknowledging real limits.

Tom Barnosky, a Stanford biologist whose work involves using fossil records to map changes in ecosystems over time, has reported that extinction rates today are moving at roughly one hundred times the rate typically seen in Earth's four-billion-year known history of supporting life.[4] Such rapid population loss means that the earth is currently experiencing the worst mass extinction episode since the dinosaurs. The Intergovernmental Science-Policy Platform on Biodiversity and Ecosystem Services (IPBES) estimates that over a million species of animal and plant life are now threatened by extinction. According to the World Wildlife Fund's *Living Planet Report 2020*, there has been a 68 percent drop in the global population of amphibians, birds, fish, mammals and reptiles between 1970 and 2016. And nearly 40 percent of plants are at risk of extinction. Biologist E. O. Wilson argued that the loss of species is what future generations will most judge us for. Species that disappear cannot be replaced; there is no option for remediation.

How could we be so blind? Part of the answer lies in the same factors we encountered with climate change—in particular the absence of responsibility

---

[4]   This is a low estimate. Other scientists have suggested that the more accurate number is 1,000 to 10,000 times higher than the natural extinction rate.

and foresight, and a failure to acknowledge fundamental limits. But with species extinctions, we add a particularly direct influence: the disconnection from nature that comes with Transition. The result is a failure to understand the systemic relationships that exist throughout nature, and a lack of motivation to take our relationship with nature seriously.

I think of the extinction crisis as a particularly tragic example of stopping-short Transitional Absurdity. The fact that it affects not just us but the well-being of life on earth as a whole makes it particularly inexcusable. Our children know this. At a deeper level than most people realize, this fundamental moral failing contributes to today's Crisis of Purpose.

The Fact of Real Limits

I've tied the concept of Transitional Absurdity to the need for new human capacities. Environmental challenges bring particular attention to one of the most important of these: maturity in our relationship with limits. We can avoid environmental catastrophe only if we accept that there are certain things that we simply cannot continue to do; and that there are real limits to what we as humans can understand and control.

Because the need for a mature relationship to limits is so fundamental to effectively addressing concerns of all sorts, it deserves a closer look. This need links directly to the need in our time for a wholly new kind of narrative, and it also put Cultural Maturity's task in historical perspective.

Modern Age stories juxtapose two kinds of narratives: heroic and romantic—each finding its power in the assumption that limits exist to be transcended. While heroic narratives describe overcoming obstacles to realize some ultimate achievement, romantic narratives describe some meeting—either personal or more encompassing—that results in emotional or spiritual completion. The most familiar social narratives—the American Dream, opposing political worldviews, the traditional beliefs of our various religions, progress's promise of ever onward-and-upward scientific discovery and technological advancement—are all of this heroic/romantic sort.

The need for a new maturity in relationship with limits is a new capacity that I have written about extensively.[5] Both heroic and romantic narratives fail us when we look to the future. While each of these stories celebrates limitlessness, in our time the key to moving forward is the acknowledgement of real limits. The new, more "grownup" relationship with limits comes into play not just with environmental limits, but with every part of our personal and collective lives.

We see it personally in the way we need to fundamentally rethink identity. Any deep understanding of identity requires that we acknowledge limits to what we can know, even about ourselves. We confront it, too, with what is required to make love work in our time. Culturally mature love requires recognizing limits to what one person can be for another. It is also necessary to effectively address moral questions of all sorts. Central to culturally mature moral perspective is the recognition that moral questions in the end are not about good versus evil, but about competing goods. I've also written about the importance of addressing limits more collectively if we are to have effective government or health care delivery systems. And we need to do so if we are to effectively assess risk with regard to any of the potentially existential questions of our time—not just climate change, but also pandemics, weapons of mass destruction, and the possibility that our digital technologies will be our undoing.

Failing to acknowledge real limits is one of the most common ways that stopping-short Transitional Absurdities manifest. A simple lesson summarizes what getting beyond such traps requires of us. Prior to our time, when we encountered limits, we assumed that our task was to heroically (or romantically) break through them. With Cultural Maturity, we first pause and take time to discern just what kind of limit we face. If it is a limit that warrants a more traditional response, we proceed as before, and with added conviction. But we

---

5   See Charles M. Johnston, MD, Cultural Maturity: A Guidebook for the Future, ICD Press, 2018.

are also open to the possibility that the limit is inviolable. In a culturally mature reality, making this kind of distinction becomes a central task of leadership in all parts of our personal and collective lives.

Integrative Meta-perspective fundamentally changes our relationship to limits. It makes clear that recognizing where real limits exist is one of the necessary first steps if we wish to engage any question in a culturally mature way. Historically, this would be interpreted as failure or weakness. But from Cultural Maturity's more systemic vantage, the fact of limits becomes obvious, and obviously important to always consider. The recognition of inviolable limits becomes key to success and the making of wise—and thus ultimately powerful—choices.

The Selling of Pseudo-Significance

Some of our times' most dangerous stopping-short Transitional Absurdities are products of today's Crisis of Purpose and the way it leaves us vulnerable to exploitation. When we lack a deep sense of significance in our lives, we become easy targets for pseudo-significance. This dynamic amplifies dramatically how Transition distances us from bodily experience and from the more foundational aspects of who we are.

The selling of pseudo-significance is not new, and it continues to manifest all around us. We encounter it with ads that promise, if only we buy this or that product, our lives will be complete. We find it in "if it bleeds it leads" journalism that attempts to convince us that the latest shooting or disaster in some distant place is the most worthy topic for our attention. And we see it with the growing proliferation of "click bait" and "fake news." Information has become like professional wrestling: manufactured mayhem masquerading as purpose. I think of the selling of pseudo-significance as one of the most consequential and pervasive manifestations of Transitional Absurdity. It is becoming so common that we fail to recognize that anything dubious is happening.

Decades ago, I wrote a piece to raise an alarm about the selling of pseudo-significance. After seeing a movie that had been positively reviewed, I came away feeling deeply disturbed. I realized that its content existed primarily as a vehicle for endless shootings and explosions. I was disturbed in part because I could see how this dynamic could contribute to our epidemic of gun violence; but I was more disturbed by the selling of pseudo-significance. The movie was, in effect, a Skinner box in which artificial neural stimulation was masquerading as meaning. A colleague responded to my article by saying this was increasingly what movies had become.

Over recent decades, this kind of Transitional Absurdity has progressively become the norm. We find a particularly significant manifestation with our addiction to electronic devices. The repeated shootings, explosions, and flashing images prevalent in video games can translate into almost pure artificial stimulation in the name of meaning—with repeated jolts of "meaning" coming in ever larger doses. The result is a totally reliable excitement to which young boys can be highly vulnerable. For many people, particularly girls, it is social media that provides the more insidious expression of this dynamic. Nearly 60 percent of teen girls today—twice the number found in teen boys—report feeling persistently sad and hopeless,with social media the likely culprit. Here the artificial substitute for meaning tends to be emotional. While there can be productive applications of social media, the very real dangers are increasingly being recognized.

In each case, the harm comes back to how effective our electronic devices are as mechanisms for selling pseudo-significance. It has been a dirty secret of high-tech companies that they were optimizing programs for these addictive effects, but we would have this addictive result even without their efforts. Simple optimization depends on hijacking our attention—a dynamic that is multiplied many times over by the fact that sites are advertisement driven. Addiction is a much more reliable way to get attention than providing content that benefits us.

The obvious harm being done is only one part of the Transitional

Absurdity I see regarding our attachment to our electronic devices.. Another contributor is the length of time it has taken us to recognize the damage and its implications. When social media first came on the scene I wrote about my concerns. There is nothing more precious and central to meaning than our attention. That we would let technologies that so directly hijack our attention go unchecked, and in fact celebrate them, reflects a particularly egregious kind of blindness. We have to ask how we could have let it happen.

And we likely haven't seen the worst of such effects. New advances in machine learning amplify these addictive dynamics in ways that we cannot control or often even understand. George Orwell, in his dystopian novel *1984* warned of Big Brother taking control of our minds. The real danger in the future may not be government manipulation, but artificial stimulation masquerading as substance, and information being used in ways that ultimately disconnects us from real importance. It is a topic I will return to with our look at techno-utopian, overshooting-the-mark Transitional Absurdities in Chapter Five.

Rethinking Wealth and Progress

This particularly encompassing issue points toward an area where growth is required if we are to get beyond today's crisis of narrative. In the final analysis, our human well-being will depend on a fundamental redefining of wealth and progress. This is another conclusion that I and many others wrote extensively about decades back, and it becomes obvious with any close examination. Even so, it is an idea that many people today still can hardly get their heads around. I think of this absence of needed big-picture perspective as a particularly consequential example of stopping-short Transitional Absurdity.

Our modern age definitions are so familiar that we tend to accept them without question. We define wealth as the accumulation of material assets, and progress the combination of new inventions and economic growth; but neither of these definitions can work going forward. If we don't question these definitions—and question them fundamentally—the consequences will be dire. We can think of denial in the face of this most basic of challenges as a particularly defining kind of stopping-short Transitional Absurdity.

The topic in another way helps put the concept of Transitional Absurdity in historical perspective and highlights its importance.

Thinking about advancement as we have during our most recent chapter in culture's story is not in itself a problem. In its time, it has greatly benefitted us. Those familiar definitions of wealth and progress have been closely tied to our modern concept of the individual and central to the achievements of the Industrial Age and the great power of modern economies. But while our familiar definitions of wealth and progress might seem logical, they are products primarily of thought from times past. They leave us short of what we will need going forward.

When I want to help people realize what more is needed, I will often first engage them at a personal level. I will ask them to tell me what creates meaning—"wealth" in the largest sense—in their individual lives. Most people mention money; but most also recognize that beyond a certain point money is less tied to meaning than one might think. Invention, too, generally has a place; people like their gadgets. But most people recognize that other things are ultimately as important, and often much more so: one's family, one's friends, one's community, one's relationship with nature, one's creative and intellectual pursuits.

People who perform this exercise are often surprised to find that a significant mismatch exists between what they have described as most important for a meaningful life and many of their day-to-day choices. I may joke with the person as they confront this recognition, pointing out—only partly tongue in cheek—that this sort of discrepancy borders on the definition of insanity. Using this exercise in therapy can result in people making major life changes.

We can apply this same kind of inquiry to the way we collectively think about advancement. When we do, it becomes hard to deny that our current world circumstances reflect a related kind of mismatch. Too often today we hold to outmoded definitions of wealth and progress that exclude much that is in fact most important to us. Just as we appropriately regard an individual as deranged who makes choices that contradict that which the person finds most important, the implications are huge.

This recognition once again becomes obvious if we simply look at what creates meaning in our lives—in this case, in our shared experience as humans. And Creative Systems Theory lets us be more specific. As I have described with the Dilemma of Trajectory, clinging to the modern age narrative beyond its time threatens to distance us from much that matters to us. The result could be not merely painful, but our undoing as a species.

In every part of our lives, systemically conceived measures of advancement are becoming essential. For example, if we are to successfully assess the benefits and risks of new technologies, systemically inclusive measures will be required. (Without them we have no way to know what we are to call a "benefit.") Systemically inclusive measures will similarly be critical to making good environmental decisions. (It is only through systemically inclusive measures that we can appreciate the extent to which further environmental destruction would impoverish us.) And, certainly, more mature and systemic measures for wealth and progress will be necessary if we are to effectively address the ever-widening gap between the world's haves and have-nots. (Asking about benefit more consciously allows us to recognize how such disparities not only are ethically troubling, but also risk destabilizing societies and putting everyone's well-being in peril.)

These should not be viewed as radical observations; they are just common sense. That the importance of rethinking wealth and progress has not become a major front-page-news topic makes it an ultimate example of stopping-short Transitional Absurdity. Fortunately, we may now be making a start. For example, the Wellbeing Economic Governments Partnership (WEGO), including Finland, Iceland, Scotland, Wales, and New Zealand (with others set to join), recently came together with the express aim of transforming economies around the world to deliver shared well-being for the people and planet. In the words of Scotland's former First Minister Nicola Sturgeon, "The need for a new economic model had never been clearer."

If our concern is the long-term well-being of the species, no task is more important than defining wealth and progress in more complete and life-affirming ways. The courage to do so in our time will be what most determines whether the choices we make today are sane and ultimately beneficial.

CHAPTER THREE

Reactive Transitional Absurdities: Polarization and Regression

The second kind of Transitional Absurdity involves protective responses to our time's considerable demands. It is this kind of Transitional Absurdity that is most likely to grab our attention and alert us to the fact that we may be seeing something more than just ordinary confusions and differences. When systems risk being overwhelmed—or, expressed in Creative Systems terms, when circumstances require more than their available Capacitance—they may respond reactively in order to distance themselves from the "offending" challenge. Two of the most common such protective responses to the challenges of our times, and specifically to the challenges presented at Transition, are polarization and regression.

Here we will start by looking more closely at the extreme polarization we find today in response to questions of almost every sort. In particular we give attention to how polarization manifests not only in differences of opinion, but also in polarization at the level of cognitive structures. We will touch briefly on how we have seen regression on multiple fronts in recent decades. We will look at specific concepts that help us recognize polarization and understand how it relates to the challenges presented by Cultural Maturity. And we will examine examples that illustrate how such understanding can help us move forward in our thinking.

Polarization

Our growing social and political polarization is a major concern. In recent decades, we've seen reactive polarization become ever more pronounced and people's voices ever shriller. With issues of every sort, people today are dividing almost immediately into polar camps. Often with particular issues it is not at all clear that there is any reason for conflict. All we know is that division will happen eventually and result in absolutist advocacy on both sides. Conflict between ideological factions has become so pronounced that real conversation about many topics has become largely impossible.

In response to the concerning situation, in 2021 I wrote a book titled, *Perspective and Guidance for a Time of Deep Discord.* I expected that the book would quickly find a grateful audience, given how much of an obstacle polarization had become. However, the book has not done particularly well. In talking to people who read it, I discovered the apparent reason. Given the nature of the problem, it made sense; but it took me by surprise. Most people recognize that polarization is not a good thing, but they assume that the problem lies in some "other side" doing the polarizing. They miss the point that the problem is polarization itself. If the problem is some polarizing "other side," then we should expect the book to be trivial, to tell us nothing we don't already know.

People always have had differences, but the reactive, absolutist polarization we see today is new. And it is of major concern if we are to get along and have effective governance. Of particular pertinence to the topic of Transitional Absurdity is the fact that extreme polarization makes culturally mature understanding essentially impossible.

A couple of observations relate specifically to this book's reflections. The first concerns the question of exactly what we are seeing with these circumstances. It brings attention to the essential recognition that we are dealing not only with the fact that different people can reach different conclusions, but also with a fracturing of our cognitive mechanisms. The second turns to the essential question of why we see what we do. My answer is tied to truth-related observations I've made with regard to the concept of Capacitance, and also to earlier descriptions of the dynamics of Transition.

Let's start with the "what we see" insight. The important recognition is that today's increasing political and social polarization alerts us to the fact that it has less to do with what we think than *how* we think. Ultimately it is about something more basic even than collections of beliefs and values, what has been called "worldview," though that gets us a bit closer. What we witness reflects polarized psychological patterns; or, more precisely, patterns of cognitive organization. It is not so much that belief is creating polarization, but that polarity's role in how we think is creating polarized belief.

Most people will find it surprising that the notion that social/political polarization has more to do with our cognitive mechanisms than the real complexities of policy. We tend to think of our opinions as rationally derived conclusions. And the media tends to take people's utterances at face value, that what they say is generally what they mean, or at least that the words adequately reflect what drives their concerns. But the recognition that we are dealing with underlying cognitive patterns is key. It is critical to explaining why getting beyond polarization can be so difficult, and why efforts at civil discourse so often fail. And if the concept of Cultural Maturity is accurate, this recognition is essential to understanding what is needed going forward.

The particulars of belief can in fact be products of reasoned consideration. And beliefs can be influenced by numerous external factors: where we live (urban versus rural, for example), the family we grew up in, and the unique challenges our particular life may present. But when belief takes the form of ideology, we see psychological patterns. We can think of these patterns as "ecological niches" in the makeup of our psyches. Different social narratives fit most comfortably into certain cognitive niches.

Some of the best evidence that today's extreme social and political polarization has less to do with *what* we think than *how* we think can be found in the common intractableness of people's opinions. We tend to assume that when people have views different from our own, the appropriate response is to engage in reasoned discussion and debate. But in fact debate rarely changes anyone's mind, often resulting in positions becoming even more entrenched.

We find further evidence when issues that are not thought of in partisan terms when first they come to the public's attention, later become highly polarized. This was the case, for example, with both climate change and health care reform. There were no obvious sides to the climate change debate when the evidence first came to light; and Obamacare was initially modeled after Republican Mitt Romney's plan in Massachusetts.

We find additional evidence in the frequent closeness of elections. If voting were based on the perceived intelligence of a candidate and his or her ideas, we would much more often see general agreement as to which candidate is the most qualified. Instead, elections typically are won by a few percentage points—sometimes very few. This is exactly what we would predict if we were dealing not with mere differences of opinion, but with opposite polarized cognitive patterns. Pushed to extremes, polarities split fifty-fifty, like two sides of a coin. One of the best ways to win an election if you are not really qualified is to create controversy and polarization. Because polar opposites tend to split approximately evenly, you should then be able to win close to half of the vote.

More evidence that polarization is a result of how, not what we think is the almost inverse relationship that exists between the degree to which a person is informed and the likelihood that he or she will have strong views. If surety was a product of how thoroughly topics had been researched, we would expect the opposite. But commonly we find the most strident views and the lengthiest pronouncements from people who in fact know the least, and have least to offer to a conversation. Less information maintains cognitive patterns; more information risks internal dissonance.

It turns out that we can make fairly accurate predictions about the ideological beliefs that we will encounter, by teasing apart psychological structures and patterns[6] and making use of sufficiently nuanced conceptual tools. We can then predict underlying values more than particular opinions, an observation that can prove immensely useful. At the least, it helps make sense of otherwise confusing results—such as the way people can have views that seem to belie their best interest, or how we so often find strange-bedfellow alliances. It also helps us appreciate what the encompassing understanding that comes with culturally mature systemic perspective involves, and what it requires of us.

The second topic is equally worthy of our attention and particularly pertinent to this book's inquiry. I gave my book *Perspective and Guidance for a Time of Deep Discord* the subtitle: *Why We See Such Extreme Social and Political Polarization—and What We Can Do About It*. Interestingly, I have an easier time identifying solutions than confidently providing explanation. In the book, I describe in detail the backsliding over the last twenty or thirty years that I've briefly noted here. I also admit that it is not clear to me why we are seeing it.

But, uncertainties acknowledged, the question of why we witness what we do is definitely important. The consequences could be very different with different answers to that question. And, depending on our answer, what is being asked of us could also be very different. With several explanations, major changes (at least in the short term) may not be needed. But as I have noted, there are also reasons to think we may be dealing with dynamics of a more fundamental sort.

It is quite possible that the extreme polarization we witness today is not of great concern. I noted in Chapter One that it simply could be a product of the common two-steps-forward-one-step-back nature of societal change. It is also possible that what we see could follow from dynamics more particular to our time, but which nevertheless have familiar antidotes. Today's extreme views might reflect momentary regression in the face of many demanding challenges.

---

[6]   See Charles M. Johnston, MD, The Creative Systems Personality Typology, ICD Press, 2023.

I've described how human systems by nature will often polarize and regress when confronted with demands that threaten to overwhelm them—when they are pushed beyond their available Capacitance. However, if the challenges are temporary and the overwhelm is not that great, patience and perspective should be all that is needed to take care of things—at least if we can avoid making destructive choices in response to feeling overwhelmed.

Still, what we are seeing could in fact be a consequence of overwhelming challenges; and, with them, a more pronounced and less easily addressed regression. Many of today's critical concerns—for example, globalization, climate change, job loss through automation, dramatic changes created by the information revolution, the growing gap between the world's haves and have-nots, and the loss of familiar cultural guideposts in so many areas of our lives—are specifically new and could result in a particularly severe experience of overwhelm.

Importantly, there is an observation hidden in these descriptions with particular pertinence to the concept of Transitional Absurdity and the legitimacy of hope. While it doesn't make things easier, if it is accurate it does alter the possible implications. Aspects of this easily overwhelming picture—the loss of familiar guideposts in many areas of our lives, for instance—may be products of Cultural Maturity-related changes. The demands that come with Cultural Maturity's "growing up"—including taking greater responsibility in our choices, better tolerating life's real uncertainties and complexities, and more effectively dealing with real limits—require that we face realities that before now we could not have tolerated. If such demands are playing a major role in current circumstances, this would further increase what our times require of us—considerably. But it would also increase the likelihood that we can get through these difficult times. It would mean that what overwhelms us now may be, in the end, what will be required to save us. Today's backsliding could be part of an awkward, in-between time in a predicted developmental process.

In this book I note kinds of evidence, beyond just the nature of the challenges we face, that support the idea that Cultural Maturity's changes may play a role in what we are seeing. I describe, for example, how the fact that today we find polarization not only between historically common competing forces, but also between alternative, extreme populist ideologies, is consistent with the notion that what we are seeing is a form of Transitional Absurdity. This is something we should expect to find at the peak of Transition.

At this point, we can know two things for sure. First, whatever their origins, today's extreme social and political polarization directly puts us at risk. The critical nature of so many of the challenges that we now confront means that such deep divisions present real dangers. Second, whatever the cause, what is being called for is ultimately the same: the ability to understand our worlds in more mature and encompassing ways. This is the case even if the challenge is only to weather the effects of more particular stressors. But it is especially true if Cultural Maturity's demands are playing a significant role in what we see. Specific policy approaches could have an impact; for example, anything that addresses today's growing economic disparities could lessen populist tensions. And, in the short term, we may get away with simply finding ways to better get along. But, with time, the need for the more integrative change that comes with Cultural Maturity's cognitive reordering should become inescapable.

Regression

Regression reflects another way systems can protect themselves in the face of potential overwhelm. Go back to the realities of an earlier time, and the offending challenges in effect disappear. This is something we see today on multiple fronts.

Previously I described the backsliding we've witnessed over the last thirty years. I noted the Catholic nun who shared with me her disappointment that ecumenical conferences common in the later decades of the last century (which brought together people from far-flung faiths) had become rare. And I reflected on related backsliding in my own field of psychiatry and in the political sphere. Of particular pertinence to current political polarization, I noted that, thirty years ago, books and newsletters that attempted to articulate post-partisan political perspective were much more common than they are today.

It is important to recognize that regressive dynamics over recent decades have spanned the globe. They are most readily visible in the increasing influence of authoritarian sensibilities. With countries where democracy was not well-established, we have more often seen authoritarian rulers prevail—such as in Hungary, Turkey, the Philippines, Syria, Sudan, and Nicaragua. The promise of an Arab Spring in the Middle East proved to be premature. And authoritarian changes can have global implications. We've witnessed Vladimir Putin behaving more in keeping with Cold War sensibilities—even those of Stalin or the czars. We've also seen the influence of China's expressly authoritarian government grow on the world stage.

At once, we find established democracies attacked from within, often by politicians willing to damage the very institutions that brought them to power. The January 6, 2021, storming of the U.S. Capitol provides the most visible example. Freely elected leaders, in Brazil and India, for example, have taken antidemocratic actions that undermine established institutions.

In 2022, Freedom House[7] reported sixteen consecutive years of decline in global freedom (Figure 3-1). According to the same report, a total of sixty countries suffered declines over the past year, while only twenty-five improved. Some 38 percent of the global population live in countries that Freedom House views as unfree—the highest proportion since 1997. Only about 20 percent of the world now live in what it considers free countries.

---

7   From the Freedom in the World 2022 report at www.freedomhouse.org.

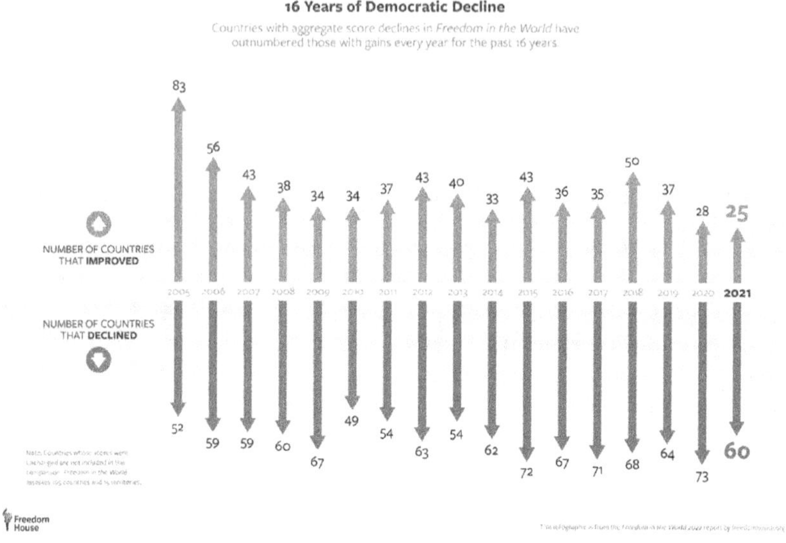

Fig. 3-1 Sixteen Reported Years of Decline in Global Freedom

However, popular demand for democracy remains strong, and people continue to risk their lives to support freedom in their countries. Many others undertake dangerous journeys in order to find places where they can live freely. But it is also the case that today we see clear challenges to the progress made by democratic rule over the last century.

As with polarization, it is not clear why we might witness such backsliding. Again, several explanations, including the possibility that it reflects the two-step-forward-one-step-back way societal change has typically occurred, suggest that great concern is not warranted. But I suspect that the dangers are real. At the least, such regression reflects the awkward in-between dynamics that systems manifest as they struggle to engage major change processes.

What we do know is that we need to be aware that regressive dynamics are taking place. If we aren't, we can end up depressed and disoriented. We can also respond by acting in ways that amplify the regression by further polarizing and blaming others for our pain. And beyond this there is a more embracing conclusion: the importance of that critically needed "growing up" as a species. With each of the examples I have noted, engaging culturally mature capacities provides the needed antidote to the backsliding we witness today.

Polar Fallacies and Cultural Maturity's Cognitive Reordering

The recognition that polarization has more to do with how rather than what we think invites us to look more closely at how cognitive polarization works. And the fact that the challenges presented by Cultural Maturity's changes may be playing a major role in what we see today suggests that we will find important insights in understanding polarization as a protective mechanism against Cultural Maturity's demands.

The Creative Systems concept of polar fallacies provides perspective, beginning with a couple of key recognitions. First is the fact that polarities are not just about opposing beliefs: They have an underlying cognitive symmetry. To use language from psychology, they juxtapose harder, more "archetypally masculine" characteristics, with softer, more "archetypally feminine" qualities. The second recognition is that culturally mature perspective "bridges" common polar assumptions.

Ideas that don't successfully "bridge"—and there are lots of ways this can happen—stop short of the needed maturity of understanding. Creative Systems Theory provides a framework for making highly detailed "polar trap" distinctions. But a more general kind of "polar trap" observation provides a useful and compact compare-and-contrast language for analyzing ways that our thinking may go astray.

The various ways we fall off the systemic roadway in our thinking can be divided into three basic types of polar fallacies—what Creative Systems Theory calls Separation Fallacies, Unity Fallacies, and Compromise Fallacies. We can lose our way by falling off the right side of the road, by falling off the left side, or by straddling the white line in the middle (Figure 3-2).

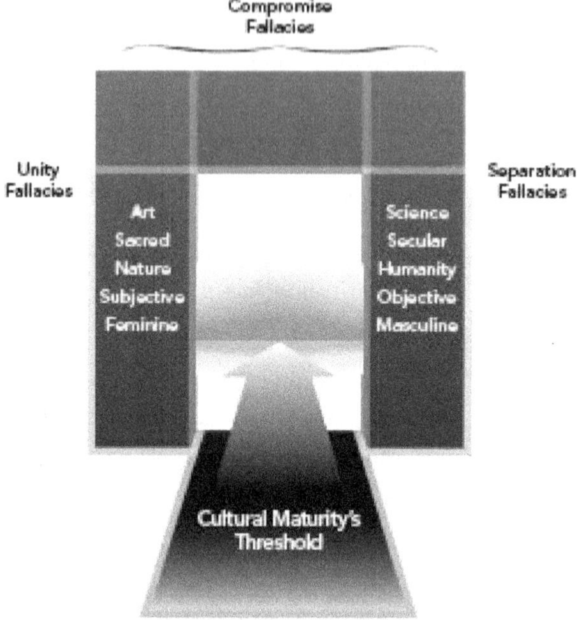

Fig. 3-2 Polar Fallacies

Separation Fallacies identify with the archetypally masculine—they fall off the right side of the conceptual roadway. They equate truth with difference, with perceived fundamental distinctions such as those between men and women, material and spiritual, intellect and emotion. And they give greatest value to the more creatively manifest side of the polarity (in these examples, men, the material, and the intellect). Some common Separation Fallacies: We are each wholly unique, individual. Experts have the answers. The final truth can be rationally articulated and objectively demonstrated. Man is separate from Nature and has rightful dominion over Her. Change is a simple product of cause and effect.

Unity Fallacies identify with the archetypally feminine and fall off the left side of the conceptual roadway. Related Unity Fallacies might include: In the end, we are all one (differences are irrelevant). The ordinary person knows best (better than leaders and institutions). The final truth is what we know from within. We are always to live in accord with Nature. Everything happens for a reason, even if that reason remains mysterious (everything is connected). Unity Fallacies argue against distinction and emphasize oneness. They may claim a transcendence of polarity, but in fact they very specifically take a side. They give their allegiance to the softer, more creatively germinal hand of creation—to the spiritual over the material, feelings over facts, the timeless over the specific.

Compromise Fallacies split the difference. A few related Compromise Fallacies are: We are all different in our own ways ("different strokes for different folks"). Good decisions result from everybody having an equal say. There are many kinds of truth and each has its merits. Nature can be different things to different people. In the end, life is what we make of it. Some Compromise Fallacies advocate a safe, additive middle ground. Others argue for multiple options but give us nothing beyond this accurate but meager observation; they claim to address diversity but fail to address what makes differences different. Compromise fallacies take us beyond black-and-white reasoning, but in the end replace it only with shades of gray.

These are shorthand explanations: For starters, no one type of fallacy is as distinct from the others as the labels might suggest. For example, Unity Fallacies commonly carry a hidden Separation Fallacy, and Separation fallacies similarly a hidden Unity Fallacy. A person who sees his own group as chosen and a conflicting group as evil succumbs to a Unity Fallacy with regard to his compatriots and a Separation Fallacy in relation to his adversaries.

In addition, there are in fact many versions of each type of fallacy. Some correspond to certain personality styles and specific views of the future; some with others. We can talk, for example, of multiple, very different kinds of Unity Fallacies. We often see a particularly spiritual Unity Fallacy with advocates of New Age or back-to-the-land philosophies. But we also find very different Unity Fallacies with more fundamentalist religious beliefs that ally with "family values" and polarize against moral relativism and intellectual elites. Different yet are the more intellectual Unity Fallacies common in academic and liberal thought, which side with the underprivileged and polarize against conservatives and corporations. Later, we will use the Creative Function to tease apart these different types of Unity Fallacy and to clarify why we predictably find them where we do.

When we encounter one of our three basic kinds of fallacies, we may see only a product of momentary misunderstanding; but more often it reflects an underlying psychological/cognitive pattern. If we are vulnerable to polar traps, we will tend to fall in the same trap whatever question we consider. We tend to be consistent in the kinds of reactive Transitional Absurdities we are likely to fall into.

Stepping Over Cultural Maturity's Threshold

We can learn a lot by looking more closely at Transitional Absurdities of the reactive sort. They teach us how the ways we think can leave us short, and they provide insight for moving forward, particularly where the protective mechanisms involve polarization.

A simple lesson offers basic guidance when any belief becomes polarized. In times past, when we encountered polarized positions and partisan advocacy, we assumed that there were only two options and that our job was to figure out which one was right and to fight for it. But as we look to the future, polarization has very different implications. It alerts us to the fact that we have yet to ask the hard questions that ultimately need to be addressed. When we succeed at asking the larger questions, we recognize that there have always been more than just two sides. We also see that while each traditional side may hold a piece of the truth, neither side, by itself, nor some averaging of positions, can get us where we need to go.

To illustrate how this simple recognition helps us, I will touch briefly on three issues that today produce strongly polarized responses—immigration, globalization, and abortion. Each helps us understand what is going on when beliefs become reactively polarized, and each invites us to contemplate how we might systemically engage polarized issues of any sort.

The Immigration Quandary

In response to today's extreme social/political polarization, I wrote a series of articles that took front-page-news issues and addressed them from a big-picture, systemic perspective—far above the partisan fray. My intent with this series was not to get people to be kinder to each other, though that would have been a nice side benefit. Rather it was to help make clear that all sorts of questions today require of us greater maturity and perspective; if only we ask them usefully and arrive at effective answers.

I titled the following piece, "Bringing Big-Picture Perspective to the Often Pain-filled Confusions of the Immigration Debate." Besides making polarization more understandable, it helped to illustrate another new needed capacity if we are to address issues with requisite systemic maturity: the importance of taking context into account.

Attempts to craft effective immigration policy have increasingly resulted in polarized debate that goes nowhere. Often the result is not just confusion and poorly thought-out policy, but the perpetration of real harm—from both sides. From one side, short-sighted exclusionist policies can do harm to those who might seek to immigrate. Such policies also often do harm to countries that might be rewarded by the contributions immigrant populations have traditionally made in their new homes. From the other side we find people getting labeled as racist, should they assert that borders are important. While bigotry can play a role when borders are emphasized, the best of such response is not racist. Whatever the case in a particular situation, the basic observation, that attention to the kinds of borders we want is essential to good policy, is valid—and important.

What is needed if we are to have more useful debate? I think of three key recognitions. None is ultimately complicated. But each requires a nuanced perspective to fully grasp.

First, we need to think more consciously about borders and conceive of them more dynamically than in times past. A cell makes a good metaphor. Cells are alive because they have boundaries—cell membranes. Without a membrane, the cell would die. But to complete this first recognition—and the metaphor—we also need to mention a critical attribute of living boundaries: Cell membranes are "semi-permeable." If the membrane were merely a wall, the cell would die. Cells are most vital when the balance between the cells membrane's "yeses" and "noes" are just right for the context in which it finds itself. Similarly, individuals and societies are most vital and creative when the balance is "just right" for who they are and their particular situations.

The second recognition is key if our boundary-related conversations are to be at all productive. Different people, by virtue of temperament are more attuned to the "yes" or "no" aspects of any kind of boundary. A detailed look at temperament/personality is beyond our scope in this short piece, but a few simple observations provide a start. People who think of themselves as liberals are most likely to identify with the "yes" aspect of semi-permeability. "Openness" is an important value. People who think of themselves as conservative are most likely to identify with the "no" aspect of semi-permeability. They find particular importance in safety and in bonds with family and community. While they also value openness, it is openness within those bonds that is important to them. Such openness requires vigilance with regard to just who gets let in.

Either group will tend to polarize if it feels threatened—something we see increasingly with the immigration debate. From the Left we get views that denigrate anyone who might advocate for more solid borders. From the Right we find views that see openness to immigration as naive and elitist. Either position perpetrates its own kind of violence—and not just toward those who might disagree. Like the cell and its membrane, absolute openness and no openness at all are each, in the end, incompatible with life. If our border-related debates are to be at all civil—and certainly if they are to result in effective policy—we need to appreciate how the positions of each side reflect an important aspect of needed understanding.

The third recognition expands on the observation that the right kind of border policy may be very different depending on the situation. We must learn both to better tease apart how different contexts are different and to better understand how different contexts may call for different kinds of boundary relationships. A conversation I had recently with a valued colleague who lives in London highlights this further recognition. My colleague had contacted me because he felt that an article I had written that made reference to immigration policy had had an unacknowledged liberal bias. He had been a supporter of Great Britain separating from the European Union. A primary reason for that support had been that he saw the European Union unwilling to limit immigration in ways that he felt necessary for Britain's well-being. He also felt denigrated and misunderstood for his position.

It was fascinating to compare our experiences. I don't know if I would agree with my colleague if I lived in England. But I have to leave room for the possibility that I might. World circumstances with regard to the movement of populations has changed dramatically in recent decades. But I do know that I would not reach a related conclusion with regard to where I live. Immigration is central to the American story; we are a country of immigrants. And immigration in my home state of Washington has been almost wholly positive in its influence. That doesn't mean we haven't had controversy. But we would not have a thriving apple industry or a vital high-tech industry in the state if it were not for immigration (and much of it historically illegal).

What these conversations with my colleague mostly did was highlight the degree to which addressing immigration questions with any sophistication requires a keen sensitivity to context. There are no black and white rules. The border polities that will be most life-affirming depend on the circumstances— on both the where and when of needed policies

In reflecting on these three recognitions, it is important to appreciate that much of what is being asked of us is new. Being this conscious and responsible in how we think about borders is not something we are used to. We also aren't accustomed to reflecting this deeply on personality differences, and certainly on how such difference can benefit us. Similarly, we are not used to thinking this contextually, to examining how what is true in one situation may not be in another. If we fail to notice how much is new in what is being asked of us, we can easily misconstrue the task or become overwhelmed by it.

At the same time, these recognitions present what might seem a paradox. The task they describe need not be as complicated as we might assume given the controversy—and pain—that today so often accompanies the immigration debate. Each of these recognitions is ultimately straightforward. Step back sufficiently and each seems rather common sense. The difference, simply, is that this is maturity of common sense that we are only now learning to appreciate and put into action.

Global Versus Local

The following reflections are adapted from another article in the same series. I titled this one, "When Neither Globalization Nor Nationalism Work as Answers." We hear it asserted today that Putin's invasion of Ukraine means the end of the modern trend toward globalization. I certainly agree that his acts challenge it, but I believe there have been reasons all along to regard the kind of globalization we have celebrated in recent decades as a transitional phenomenon.

However, merely making globalization a "problem" stops us short. We get no closer if we assume that the solution is to go back to the more familiar realities of times past. Writers whom I respect have proposed that the task today is to remember who our friends are and who are our enemies. Again, while in part I agree, I also think things are not so simple.

In multiple ways, culturally mature perspective applauds globalization.

Global interconnections support better addressing the growing number of human challenges that require planetary solutions (such as climate change, epidemics, and world hunger). They also invite economic links that can be mutually beneficial. And by enhancing communication amongst people of diverse backgrounds and beliefs, globalization has the potential to support a safer and more equitable world.

But just as much, culturally mature understanding makes clear that we can't stop with globalization as we tend to think of it. This is a point I made decades ago, well before current global conflagrations. Put too much emphasis on globalization and we risk losing the unique contributions of a diverse world and the immediate sense of purpose that comes with identifications of a more local sort. Global mass culture is not an emotionally appealing outcome. And in what might seem to contradict observations in the previous paragraph, it also risks making the world a less safe place. Creative Systems Theory describes how, if the challenges a system confronts are more than it can tolerate, it will tend to polarize. Globalization alone, by overlaying cultural realities from different times in culture's story, is as likely to promote absolutist belief and inflame major conflict as it is to support cooperation.

Common ways of thinking about current circumstances have their roots in a handful of limited interpretations. On the anti-globalization side of the debate, we find identification with traditional values and nationalistic allegiances. On the pro-globalization side of the debate, people can make modern Western cultural beliefs and the global economic assumptions that follow from them ideals and end points. And the more postmodern views common in academia can assume that erasing boundaries and differences inherently provides benefit.

These contrasting ways of thinking leave us with a couple of images, neither of which can work going forward. A world of nation-states, each marking their territories and conflicting beliefs easily returns us to times when we divided the planet into allies and enemies—"chosen people" and "evil others." With today's ever more available weapons of mass destruction and challenges that require global solutions, if this is our only option, we are doomed. But if what I have described is accurate, pro-globalization positions leave us just as short. While Modern Age understanding was a grand achievement, it cannot represent an end point; and, believing it does, ultimately undermines moving forward. In the end, a postmodern world without distinctions leaves us hanging precariously, without guidance.

Creative Systems Theory offers a third image. Think of a set of nesting bowls. The globe is one bowl. A nation state is also a bowl. But there are also smaller bowls that reflect more local associations and bowls of an in-between sort that reflect regional values and alliances. In a culturally mature world, we find identification at all these circumferences. And we develop approaches to decision-making appropriate to what each requires.

This third image requires that we think well out into the future. To hold this multilayered picture, we need to be far enough along toward culturally mature understanding that we can tolerate the greater complexity, which includes the complexity of such a multi-layered picture. It also includes a further kind of complexity that I referred to in a previous article. We need to be able to tolerate and move creatively in a world in which different people's beliefs and governmental forms reflect different stages in culture's evolutionary story. But to the degree that we can do these things, we can then bring to our collective lives the best of both global and local identification.

I assume that there are other ways of imaging the future that could work. But any approach must appreciate both the gifts that come with the outward reach of globalization and the unique power and richness of the local and particular. It must also recognize the essential limits that exist on both sides of the globalization conversation. This will require foresight and creativity all the way around if our choices are to result in a healthier and safer world and not instead put us in even greater peril.

The Abortion Debate

This piece is excerpted from an article in the series, titled simply, "The Abortion Dilemma." Besides helping to fill out our understanding of polarity and its workings, it hints at approaches that can help get us where we need to go.

The abortion question reflects an essential recognition key to bringing culturally mature perspective to moral concerns more generally: that, in the end, moral dilemmas are not about good versus evil, but about competing goods. It also highlights the need to confront limits—and here, in the end, quite ultimate limits.

Abortion is an issue that we commonly associate with irreconcilable differences. But today we also find polarization becoming even more extreme. Certainly opinion has come more clearly to divide along party lines. For example, in the 1970s, Republican President Gerald Ford opposed Roe v. Wade, while both First Lady Betty Ford and Ford's vice president Nelson Rockefeller were abortion-rights supporters. Today we have seen the repeal of Roe v. Wade by the U.S. Supreme Court; and the abortions battle continues at the state level throughout the county.

Abortion is an issue where people today rarely succeed in finding common ground. But precisely because the abortion question so quickly splits people into opposing camps, it has a lot to teach us. Consulting work I did a few years ago with a social services organization provided a way in.

Abortion had become a hot-button issue in the organization, and contentious feelings were getting in the way of people working together effectively. I introduced a method that I call "Parts Work," which I often use with groups that are experiencing internal conflicts or where a group is dealing with controversial issues.

When working in this way, I start by having individuals or small subgroups represent the competing voices. A second group, sitting separately from them, assumes the role of the Whole-Person/Whole-System (culturally mature perspective) chair. People in this second group are given a sequence of tasks. First, they engage the advocate groups in conversation to clarify the divergent positions. They then converse among themselves and seek larger ways of thinking. Finally, they attempt to articulate conclusions and describe how these larger ways of understanding might translate into right and timely action.

In working with the organization, I began by separating out two small groups to speak for the pro-life and pro-choice positions. (To make things more interesting, I switched the groups so that people in each group had to argue for a position opposite to what they believed. I then had people who held those positions act as consultants, to help the advocates effectively make their arguments.) The rest of the participants—those tasked with finding larger perspective—sat in a circle outside the advocate groups.

To start the process, the two small groups spoke in turn (with the consultants coaching so the advocates didn't miss important points). The main arguments were those we commonly hear. The pro-life group argued that abortion was murder. The pro-choice group countered that the decision should be in the hands of the woman (or the woman and her doctor).

Next, I invited people in the outer circle to ask curiosity questions. Initially, their task was simply to clarify positions (the process allowed no debate at this point). While this helped increase understanding, it failed to alter the conversation. The positions of the two groups continued to appear mutually exclusive.

The people in the outer circle then took on the further task of attempting to engage the issue of abortion more systemically. Initially I had them talk quietly in pairs; with time they were to share together and do their best to articulate their conclusions. While the outer group's efforts didn't provide final answers, their reflections gradually moved the conversation from a debate about right and wrong to interactions that acknowledged legitimate feelings on both sides.

Several contributions proved particularly useful in this regard. A man who leaned more pro-choice offered that he found it impossible to escape that abortion was in fact a kind of killing—that at the least it was the ending of a potential life. He briefly apologized to his pro-choice colleagues that they might not be happy with his conclusion, but he quickly went on to suggest that denying this reality was only hiding from the real question and made real conversation impossible. And in the end, it simply left out what he felt was an essential fact.

A woman who leaned more pro-life at first also apologized, observing that while what she had to offer had helped her, others might find it too philosophical. She described how she had found herself questioning whether death was the right way to think about the opposite of life. She struggled to find words that might express a better way of thinking about it. Eventually she proposed that maybe instead of being pro-life in a literal sense, people needed to think instead in terms of what most ultimately honored life. And while she wasn't quite sure what she meant, she also offered that being sure that life endured might not be the only way to do so. Several of her colleagues countered that such semantics accomplished nothing—that death could not be consistent with life—but the observation did invite people to begin to stretch their assumptions.

Conversations continued for about an hour, going back and forth between the two advocacy groups and the people tasked with finding a larger picture. Rarely was there full agreement; but the stated goal—of generating greater mutual respect—was gradually achieved. People were able to get to the place where productive conversation at least became possible.

I've noted that the abortion question provides a prime example of the need to think in terms of competing goods. It pits the sanctity of life against a woman's right to choose. Each is clearly a good—and an important kind of good. People aren't used to thinking in terms of competing goods. And the task is compounded by a further circumstance that we commonly find with thorny issues: Each position advocates for a very different kind of good. Caught with such apples-and-oranges considerations, we confront major difficulties not just because different people may value one good as opposed to the other. Because we are dealing with wholly different concerns, there is no way we can meet half-way, even if we were inclined to do so. But the concept of Cultural Maturity suggests that if we can get at the larger, more systemic question that underlies the polar debate, we can at least make a start.

What might that question be with the abortion debate? Traditionally, the defining question with abortion concerns when life begins. Those of more conservative bent will claim it begins at conception—or at least at the time of a first fetal heartbeat. Those of more liberal inclination will tend to answer the question in terms of viability. But the "when does life begin" question proves much less helpful than we might imagine. Because each answer is in its own way legitimate, there is no clear justification for choosing one over the other. The viability answer also confronts the fact that as medical science has improved, this measure has become a moving target.

There is in fact a larger question that can begin to take us forward, one we heard hints of in the responses of each of the outer-circle contributors in the group Parts Work example. This better question asks what choices are ultimately most life-affirming, specifically in the sense of supporting life as something we experience as meaningful. This is the question that all moral concerns come back to when viewed systemically. This kind of determination is less objective. It is not something we can discern at a safe arm's length. And people can continue to disagree in how they answer it. But arguably it gets more directly at what is important.

Framing the question in this way at least begins to provide a basis for conversation. Note that at the same time it both supports and challenges the positions of both Right and Left (it presents yeses and noes to each side). For the Right, it affirms that the mere fact of life is a "good" (the yes). But at once it requires acknowledging both that the question of when life begins is open for debate; and that existence is not the only criterion for a meaningful life (the no). For the Left, the larger question supports the importance of a woman's right to choose (the yes in this exercise). But at the same time, it requires the Left to acknowledge that abortion does in fact end a possible life (the complementary no).

Merely identifying a more systemic way of thinking doesn't necessarily provide an answer that will be acceptable for everyone. Few people will find this way of framing the abortion question wholly satisfying. We can think of the reason for this in terms of any of the needed new skills and capacities I've noted in other articles. Certainly, framing the abortion question more systemically confers new responsibility, and of the ultimate sort I've pointed toward. It makes us newly responsible not just for choosing correctly, but for the truths on which we base our choices. From a culturally mature perspective, we see that accepting this greater responsibility becomes part of what it means to be moral in our time. But taking this level of responsibility in the truths we draw on is not something we are used to doing.

It is also the case that we can't really approach the abortion question more systemically without confronting the need for each of the more specific new skills and capacities I have noted. We need to accept the fact that choices are complex. And inevitably we need to acknowledge that the act of choosing involves uncertainty. Like it or not, too, we find real limits, at least with regard to the usefulness of more ideological ways of thinking; but also ultimately to what anyone can know for sure. We also again confront the fact of truth's contextual relativity. How we might answer the abortion question is going to be influenced by the degree to which we can tolerate a more systemic picture and manifest these new skills and capacities. It can also be influenced by personality style. And how abortion is viewed can be very different depending on life circumstances, such as religious background.

We again encounter the essential paradox that we find with other issues. Addressing a question like abortion with the needed apples-and-oranges sophistication requires thinking in ways that are more demanding and detailed than we are used to. Yet, at the same time, there are ways it is ultimately straightforward. Nothing defines us more than the fact that we are alive, and alive in the particularly free and creative way that makes us human. In the end, reconciling the abortion debate is about making life in that sense our measure.

CHAPTER FOUR

Overshooting the Mark Transitional Absurdities

In the transition from Modern Age realities into Cultural Maturity's needed next cultural chapter, many of the most consequential Transitional Absurdities reflect overshooting the mark. This is pretty much how things work at any major cultural change point—partly because we may fail to recognize that anything new is involved; partly as a result of fear; partly because systems are not homogeneous. When we overshoot the mark, mechanisms that previously have served us become amplified and distorted. These Transitional Absurdities take cultural change's historical trajectory and extend it onward and upward. They deny that anything like the Dilemma of Trajectory exists. In their extreme forms, they put forward images of ultimate realization.

By overshooting the mark, we can fail to question quite insane behaviors and beliefs. Here I'll start by addressing three versions. The first takes familiar ideological beliefs from the Modern Age and extends them into the future as ultimate solutions. The second mythologizes the technological, making it not just a final solution, but in important ways truth itself. And the third takes the faint remnants of left-hand, archetypally feminine sensibilities that we find with Transition and uses them for right-hand, archetypally masculine ends.

Next, I'll turn to ways in which dynamics that come with overshooting-the-mark Transitional Absurdities can be exploited, in the process amplifying the absurdity. I'll then address how overshooting the mark can manifest not only in vertical "onward and upward" dynamics, but also in a horizontal progression toward the surface layers of experience. And finally we will look at how a deep engagement with intelligence's creative multiplicity offers an antidote to overshooting-the-mark Transitional Absurdities in all its forms.

Extreme Ideological Absolutism

A common form of overshooting-the-mark Transitional Absurdity takes familiar ideological beliefs and exaggerates them to the point of ludicrousness. These may be political beliefs, philosophical beliefs, or religious/spiritual beliefs. Often the basic belief worked well as an aspect of the mosaic of understanding that intersected in modern times; but the conclusions reach Transactional Absurdity when we treat them not just as absolute truths, but as all-defining, ultimate truths.

We encounter such overshooting-the-mark assumptions with the increasing extremes of social and political polarization that we examined in the previous chapter. People have always held strong political beliefs, even to the point of making them final truths. But most often they've also recognized that debates between conflicting beliefs were part of what made democracy work: Our political structures have been designed precisely to support such debate. With today's extreme social and political polarization, however, we see something different. A growing number of people see their polar positions as truth itself; and the views of others who might disagree, the opposite of truth. People assume that if differing views could simply be eliminated, all would be well. Extended into the future, views become not just absolutist and dogmatic, but utopian.

Ideological overshooting-the-mark absurdities can take other forms besides the political. For example, we also find philosophical versions. While all philosophy has been a rational enterprise—an attempt to use logic to get at the truth—we also encounter views that extend Age of Reason's elevating of the rational such that rationality becomes truth itself. We see this with science that collapses into a narrow scientism; and with the arguments of some atheists who reduce to a kind of rational fundamentalism.[8] At the end of this chapter, I'll return to a recognition at the heart of Creative Systems Theory, that intelligence in human systems has multiple aspects, each of which is important to the kind of thinking the future will require. Miss this larger picture and our conclusions will be limited at best, and quite often destructive.

Spiritual utopian views such as New Age beliefs or extreme versions of traditional religions can be thought of in a similar way. In a limited sense, views that considered spiritual beliefs as ultimate truth have always existed. But with the challenge to Capacitance that comes with our increasingly global world, we can be less open to a plural reality. I think of contemporary Islamic fundamentalism and its expression in global terrorism in this way. Today we find resurgences of absolutist beliefs at the fringes of almost every kind of religious tradition.

Techno-Utopian Absurdities

The Modern Age onward-and-upward story is represented today in techno-utopian notions that embody more than just some rational extensions of Industrial Age and Scientific Age achievements. Assuming that future inventions will save us, they mythologize the technological, in effect making it our god. When we adopt techno-utopian thinking, we become vulnerable to a series of errors in understanding. Below are several of the most important.

Missing Where Answers May Ultimately Lie

People who fall for techno-utopian fallacies tend to miss how few of the really important challenges ahead are amenable to purely technological solutions. Climate change is the most obvious example. While invention has a role in addressing it, solutions will ultimately lie with changes in how we think

---

[8]   In Chapter Five I will expand on why such thinking necessarily fails.

and the choices we make. The same ultimately holds for avoiding nuclear catastrophe; guaranteeing adequate food, clean air, and fresh water for the world's people; addressing the dangerously growing gap between the world's haves and have-nots; or slowing the ever-increasing rate of species extinctions. None of these questions has a technological fix.

A Failure to Recognize Truly Existential Threats

We can think of our slowness in responding to the climate crisis as our failure to recognize the implications of a truly existential risk. We can also explain our lack of preparedness for the Covid pandemic in this way. While I don't see either failure as a direct product of techno-utopian assumptions, I do think that a contributing factor was a certain smugness that in our technological age, we can rise to any challenge.

The possibility that artificial intelligence could be the end of us provides what may be the most important example of existential threat. With large language and generative AI programs now on the scene, people are beginning to take notice that the dangers could be considerable. In a recent survey, AI experts were asked, "What probability do you put on human inability to control future advanced AI systems causing human extinction or similar permanent and severe disempowerment of the human species?" The median answer was 10 percent, although many experts in the field put the probability much higher. Shortly I will get back to how I see even the best of thinkers missing the danger that will ultimately put us at greatest risk, one for which I am not sure there are solutions.

If the concept of Transitional Absurdity applies, it relates to risks being accurately perceived and responded to; and if they haven't, why not. Given experts believe what they do now, the fact that we (and they) might continue to race headlong into AI development certainly raises disturbing questions.

When dangers of AI development are discussed today, we still most often focus on issues like job loss and disinformation. While these concerns are real,

I suspect they can be dealt with. Other dangers could have truly cataclysmic consequences and are not so easily addressed.

In one scenario, for example, some kind of bad actor on the world stage wages an AI-based attack on a perceived enemy. The goal could be the destruction of physical infrastructure such as electrical grids or water supplies, disruption of communications networks, or, as we have seen attempted in very rudimentary form with Russian interference in elections, a fundamental undermining of social and governmental structures. This kind of attack would not require that the perpetrator be a developed nation—only technical abilities that should become increasingly available would be needed. It could easily be mobilized by a rogue state such as North Korea or even by a terrorist group. Once initiated it could quickly spin out of control. We legitimately include this kind of application when we think of "weapons of mass destruction." In time, it may prove the most problematical example of such weaponry.

A second scenario is what people in the tech world most often point toward when they warn that AI could be the end of us. Systems that employ machine learning could very well come to outcompete us and take control. Such algorithms can be single-minded in their competitiveness in ways that we humans can never be nor would ever want to be. The fact that learning in such systems can take place autonomously and is often beyond our ability to decipher much less control means that we face the real risk of runaway mechanisms where the destruction of humanity, if not outright intentional, becomes an unintended consequence.

Of all the various existential risks that today confront us, from nuclear proliferation and climate change, to the dangerous gap between the world's haves and have-nots, a third scenario has the greatest potential to be the end of us. I introduced this danger in Chapter Two with our look at pseudo-significance and the dynamics of addiction. Increasingly our electronic devices are designed to capture our attention, and AI plays an increasing role to accomplish this. I've described how the mechanisms of device addiction are essentially the same as those of addictive drugs. Our devices create artificial stimulation that substitutes for the body's feedback that something matters. Machine learning has the potential to compound those mechanisms many times over. And of particular importance is that this result would require no ill intent.

This is not some scenario of our far-off future. We don't need recent advances like generative AI and large language models for this to occur. AI by its very nature could produce a world in which distraction and addiction replace meaningful human activity. It is essentially inevitable given the way artificial intelligence works. Imagine that you have a website, and you want to attract traffic to its content. You give an artificial intelligence algorithm the instructions to maximize the number of visitors and the time they spend there. The most reliable way to achieve this result is not to provide content that is useful, but rather to generate content that is addictive—and the more addictive, the better. AI will create ever-more effective artificial stimulation in the name of meaning, absent any additional instructions. And I know of no obvious way to stop it.

I consider the length of time it has taken people to impart high priority to AI-related concerns a pivotal example of techno-utopian Transitional Absurdity. A lot of great value can come from AI advances. But if we are at all sane, we need to be giving as much attention to identifying and responding to potential dangers as we are to development and maximizing profits. I will conclude this chapter with some thoughts about what will be required if our understanding is to be up to the task of managing this major new world of technology.

We can frame the challenge of AI in terms of assessing risk. With previous reflections of limits and climate change I drew specifically on a risk assessment frame. It is important to appreciate how easily techno-utopian thinking has us fail to adequately acknowledge risk. In our excitement with having the latest gadget, we can fail to recognize shortcomings. We may also fail to appreciate real dangers.

I'm a bit of a car guy, and a couple of car-related examples provide good illustration. The first turns to the massive touch screens that increasingly adorn new cars. Nearly every aspect of these cars' electrical functioning is controlled by what are, in effect, large cell phones or iPads. Given that touch screens have been so widely adapted, we might easily assume that they make driving simpler and safer. They do help us link to entertainment options. And car manufactures like them because they are cheaper to manufacture than physical knobs and buttons. But often, in fact, they make needed actions more complex; and there is evidence that they contribute to distracted driving, making driving less safe. The newest cars have begun to reintroduce knobs and buttons along with the screens. I suspect that the importance of doing this was not obvious from the start (it was to me) because people today mythologize their screens and associate them with the latest and coolest.

The development of self-driving vehicles presents another good example. Eventually they should help reduce not only traffic fatalities, but also roadway congestion and fuel consumption; in addition they should make time spent in traffic more tolerable. But wholly autonomous vehicles are another thing. I find it fascinating how quickly people have assumed that wholly self-driving cars are just around the corner and how little attention has been given to concerns that could be real problems. Basic advances that augment driving should eventually become commonplace; but automotive experts are beginning to realize how wholly autonomous driving will likely be much more difficult than their early, idealized vision assumed.

The concerns don't take a great deal of technical knowledge to grasp. One is simply the need for exceptional levels of reliability and safety. The software in our familiar devices is not designed to operate indefinitely without ever crashing or freezing—errors that could be deadly in a car. And we are only just beginning to appreciate the dangers that could arise if the software in self-driving cars is hacked. There is also the "hand-off" problem—how to have a person take over in an emergency when the technology encourages the person to be inattentive—an issue that is very real and not easily addressed. Even if autonomous driving were to be workable technologically, it would make getting from here to there considerably more difficult than people have assumed.

A third issue is more specifically moral. What has been called the "trolley problem" confronts us with the difficulty of programming correct choices into our "intelligent" machines. Some of those choices present major moral quandaries. Imagine you are riding along in your self-driving car and a bunch of kids run out in front of you. Your car has three options: It can swerve into traffic and quite possibly kill you. It can swerve right and collide with whatever is there—a wall, an embankment, or perhaps more pedestrians. Or it can keep going straight ahead and hit the kids. Note that the moral dilemma this situation presents is not just complex: No acceptable choice exists. We haven't given such circumstances much thought in the past because we've responded to them reactively. But if we must program them into our machines, the absence of acceptable choices becomes inescapable. Not only software engineers, but lawmakers, insurance companies, and ethicists have a lot of work to do before we have any acceptable solutions to this dilemma.

Even wholly autonomous technologies will likely have a place in the future—for example, with commercial applications on well-marked roads. My point here is only to emphasize how readily we can leave out essential factors when we idealize and mythologize technology. When risks run counter to a technological gospel's extension of the modern heroic narrative, we fall short of assessing or even recognizing them.

Failures of Priority

Techno-utopian thinking can also have us fail to think through priorities. The goal of colonizing Mars makes a good example. Space travel is the realm of human activity that in the last century has most symbolized our heroic, onward-and-upward mindset. Today the majority of people assume that colonizing Mars is a good idea and an important priority. The degree of unquestioning is both striking and informative.

The scientist in me agrees that going to Mars might be fun and that attempting to establish a colony there could be a fascinating thing to try. But the argument most often used to justify the effort—that we need to inhabit Mars as a safeguard given the damage we are doing to the earth—is really quite silly. The earth is a place where we have evolved to be perfectly adapted; Mars presents a wholly inhospitable environment. And the notion that somehow the same species that can't get along with each other or make sustainable choices on Earth can do so in such an alien place makes little sense.

It is laudable to wish to go to Mars, but not based on claims that it will save humanity. We should admit that the idea excites us because it represents a particularly dramatic and colorful extension of a kind of endeavor we find inspiring. If our concern is human survival, our energy and attention is much better spent working to assure that the earth remains healthy and hospitable for the long term. We need to find greater social maturity here on earth before we take our unsustainable beliefs to other planets.

Techno-Utopian Belief as Religion

Technological gospel beliefs can be extrapolated to the point that they become literally religious. The conclusions that result can be as delusional as those we find when any religious belief gets carried to an extreme. I think for example of the excitement about the coming "singularity"—the hypothesized point where artificial intelligence surpasses human intelligence. The notion itself is questionable for the reason I will address more directly in the concluding section of this chapter: Artificial intelligence has little to do with human intelligence. But conclusions drawn from such thinking often give away its limitations—and its spiritual associations.

Proponents talk of new forms of existence that will transcend not only our biology but also our mortality. They celebrate the possibility of digitally downloading our neurological contents to attain eternal life. That this could seem an attractive proposition reflects not just a fundamental ignorance of how intelligence works, but also a denial of limits—in this case, life's ultimate limit.

This kind of belief is best viewed as magical thinking, and a kind of magical we would expect from overshooting the mark. It extends—here to a ludicrous degree—the separation of polar opposites that has marked the historical evolution of understanding. The belief moves forward by eliminating the "offending" half of polarity, the body, in favor of an exultant (though ultimately mechanical) mind; the unconscious in favor of an all-knowing (but in fact absent of real human knowing) consciousness; and death in favor of a triumphant digital immortality. Far from being new to our time, efforts to eliminate the body, the unconscious, and death have been common to utopian beliefs for thousands of years.

Exploitative Onward and Upward Absurdities

Onward-and-upward dynamics reflect right-hand sensibilities prevailing to the point of absurdity. I've described how cultural belief has evolved over the course of history from times in which archetypally feminine sensibilities prevailed, as with tribal realities; to today, when more archetypally masculine sensibilities largely hold sway. With onward-and-upward Transitional Absurdities, this right-hand dominance is extended to such a point that we fail to question quite insane behaviors and beliefs.

Some of the most consequential of these onward-and-upward Transitional Absurdities are not so obvious as those I have previously noted. Or, more accurately, they have become so much a part of our daily lives that, like the frog who sits in the pot of gradually boiling water, unaware that it is being cooked, we tend to overlook the craziness. These absurdities involve remnants of left-hand sensibilities that remain with Transition and become coopted for right-hand ends. The left-hand value or sensibility can be of any sort—receptivity and relationship, the body, the spiritual and imaginal, nature, and more.

The coopting of today's last faint remnants of the receptive makes a good example. The word "receptive" captures the archetypally feminine at its most basic. Receptivity is about taking in. It is needed for any deep capacity to listen, for sensuality and pleasure, and for knowing what most moves us, thus understanding meaning in our lives. Yet, in spite of the fact that receptivity is so fundamental, when I use the word "receptive" today, often people barely recognize what I am talking about. They assume that the opposite of active, rather than receptive, is simply passive. The receptive is in fact as fully dynamic and significant as the active.

This situation leaves us easily exploited, in part because we are so distanced from the receptive that we can miss its significance. Equally it is because receptivity's rarity can amplify the importance even of imposters. We encounter this kind of confusion in how often people speak of today's world making us more "connected" when the opposite is frequently the case. Too easily, "likes" and "clicks" become defining measures of relationship, and "selfies" our modern signifiers of identity. In the process, receptivity and the deep connection it gives us with others and with ourselves gets highjacked. This observation provides useful further insight into the roots of addiction, whether the addicting substance is a drug, food, or the stimulation from an electronic device. Too often we lack the basic bodily feedback we need to distinguish real meaning from artificial substitutes.

There is one such dynamic that is so much a part of modern daily life that we rarely question it, although it drives much that is most concerning. It involves the effects of advertising. Many years back I wrote an article I titled "The Dilemma of Advertising—When a Time's Preeminent Art Form Undermines Truth." I described how the sensibilities that have historically produced great art make their most influential expression today in advertising. And I propose that because advertising uses art's language of image and metaphor to get us to buy things—and most often does so in ways that involve deception—the result is the antithesis of art's historical truth-telling function. This kind of Transitional Absurdity takes its most egregious form with advertising that is directed at children.

I'm sure part of the reason that I find this observation concerning has to do with my background. Before I became a psychiatrist, I was a sculptor. And I've played music through much of my life. In addition, the body of original conceptual work that defines much of my life's contribution, Creative Systems Theory, has its roots in an understanding of cognition's creative workings.

But my level of concern also comes from an appreciation of the way art historically has functioned as an indicator of where we reside in culture's story and just what is being asked of us. Think of how the art of the Renaissance presaged the later advances of the Modern Age. Creative Systems Theory proposes that the purpose of art is to highlight new ways of seeing the world. Put in Creative Systems Theory terms, art gives voice to emerging capacities in the "psyche of culture." Artistic expression tells us what is becoming true and what being aligned with the kind of truth that produces meaning will require of us.

Advertising is today's preeminent art form, if by "art" we mean activities that draw on aspects of intelligence that underly creative expression—the imaginal, the emotional, body sensibilities—certainly. And, without question, advertising is the art form on which we spend the most money. It is also that which is most pervasive around us. When businesses speak of their "creative departments," they are referring to their marketing departments.

Is this a problem? Arguably, it is wholly consistent with what I've described as art's purpose. I've noted how in modern times we have come to define wealth and progress almost exclusively in terms of economic advancement. Being that advertising's purpose is to drive economic profits, it is wholly aligned with this way of thinking about significance.

But there are many reasons for concern. The first is simply the fact that Modern Age ways of thinking about significance are no longer working. I've described how the Modern Age's individualist, materialist narrative is failing us. An art form that serves to foster it thus also necessarily fails us.

A second concern is more concrete. While there are clear ways that advertising has benefitted us, at the same time its purpose is almost the opposite of art as I have described it. Rather than a voice for possibility and emergent truth, modern advertising tends to be based on deception and manipulation. In advertising classes, one is counseled to never speak rationally about a product for the simple reason that logical consideration might *discourage* one from buying the product. Rather, ads associate fulfillment with things we don't need, often using claims that are simply not true. Advertising becomes, in effect, a form of lying.

A recent study on the proliferation of ads that boast how much you can save by changing car insurance provides an example. It found that the higher a company's advertising budgets, the *more* you were in fact likely to pay. And often the lie is directly harmful. Remember the assertion that "Salems are springtime fresh" when in fact it was well-known that cigarettes were a major health risk? And we heard the cheery mantra "Coke is It!" at the same time rates of diabetes and obesity skyrocketed. As a physician I'm deeply concerned about the growing proliferation of misleading pharmaceutical ads that make the health care provider's already difficult job even more so and contribute significantly to escalating health care costs.

Ultimately there is a deeper, even more worrying aspect of advertising's damaging effects. It concerns the way ads draw on non-rational, germinally creative aspects of intelligence that in our time we often lose touch with. Advertising tends to draw directly on the imagination at a time when, for most people, connection with the imaginal is but a faint remnant from childhood. And it implies—if only we buy the right product—levels of emotional and bodily fulfillment rarely present in most people's lives are available to us.

Because ads draw so directly on those creative parts of ourselves, we often find delight in them. I think of how many people find Super Bowl ads more interesting than the game. But precisely because they tap forgotten aspects of understanding, we should find their influence worrying—and particularly now that ads drive not just television programing, but also digital media.

This concern comes into finer focus with an appreciation for the dynamics that give us Cultural Maturity and its new ways of understanding. I've described how the cognitive changes that produce culturally mature perspective involve a new ability to at once fully step back from and deeply engage the whole of our cognitive complexity. We find the ability to engage the multiple aspects of intelligence and apply them creatively in our lives. It is this ability that makes possible the more nuanced kind of understanding—we could say the wisdom— on which our future depends.

The implications are huge if we allow the aspects of our cognitive mechanisms most needed for a deep sense of meaning to be so co-opted. We undermine our ability to take the forward steps in understanding on which our future depends. Creative Systems Theory recognizes the defining role of advertising in modern life as a prime example of overshooting the mark Transitional Absurdity.

So, what do we do? At the least, we need to recognize the manipulation and realize the depth of potential harm. When we do, advertising ceases to influence us, because it so obviously violates the purposes that the sensibilities it exploits were designed to serve.

"Horizontal" Overshooting the Mark Transitional Dynamics

These observations—about the role of the receptive and about advertising coopting the traditional function of art—point toward a recognition that helps us understand how overshooting-the-mark Transitional Absurdities work. Overshooting the mark doesn't just happen in an onward-and-upward trajectory. It also manifests horizontally, in ways that take us increasingly outward, toward the most surface layers of experience.

Creative Systems Theory maps how we can bodily understand change mechanisms. And it observes how this kind of dynamic manifests not just vertically, along the body's axis; but also horizontally, in relation to the way we experience, whether from aspects of ourselves that are more inner as opposed to more outer. Therefore we see overshooting with horizontal dynamics as well as with vertical dynamics. With transition, along with becoming ever more distanced from the ground of our being in our bodies and in nature, we also come to live more and more from the body's surface. We see such disconnects with today's obsession with physical appearance and our frequent identification with the most superficial of values. Another way of framing today's Crisis of Purpose is the recognition that today's greatest danger may be triviality.

A representation from Creative Systems Theory provides a good way to grasp this larger picture. To get there, we need to start with a way Creative Systems Theory represents the general workings of formative process (Figure 4-1). The theory describes how any human generative process—from a simple creative act to individual psychological development to the evolution of culture—has a related creative architecture. It manifests as an evolving play of polarities, from a budding from first possibilities, to a time of struggle into first crude form, to a time of finishing and polishing.

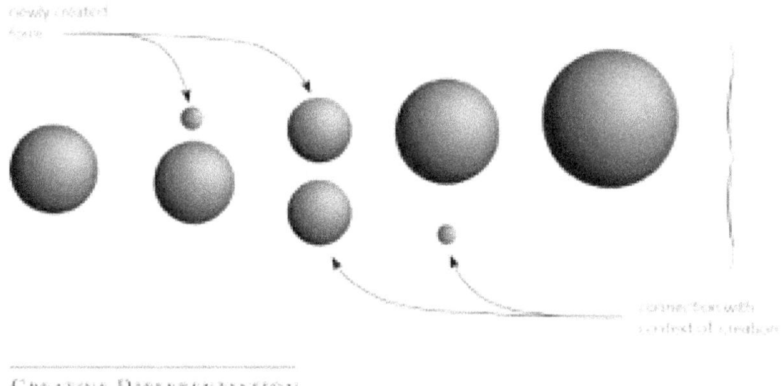

Fig. 4-1. Creative Differentiation

This generative picture is not just some abstract notion. It is reflected directly in our bodily experience. And we see it with both horizontal and vertical dynamics. Figure 4-2 depicts how horizontal polarity takes expression differently depending on when we find it. Inner aspects of experience get greater emphasis early on while Outer sensibilities later have the greater influence. Over the course of any human formative process, embodied experience moves gradually from the body's core toward the body's surface layers.

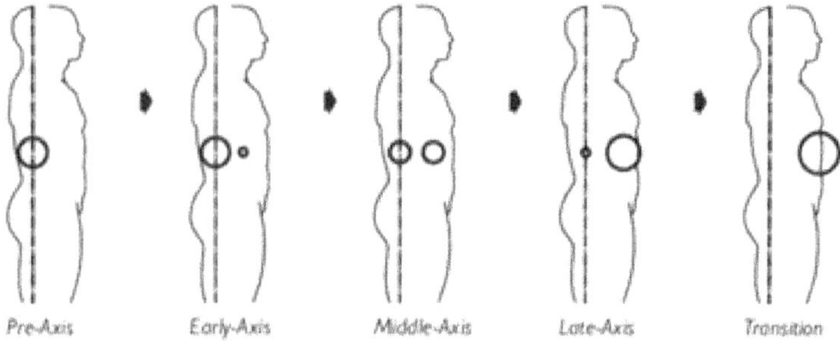

Fig. 4-2. Evolution of Horizontal Polarity[9]

Figure 4-3 adds vertical polarity to the representation. It depicts how horizontal and vertical polarity together generate our felt experience of ourselves and how we perceive our worlds.[10]

---

[9]   Here I've added the formal Creative Systems language for creative stages.

[10]   The diagrams in Figures 4-2 and 4-3 first appeared in my 1984 book, The Creative Imperative (Celestial Arts).

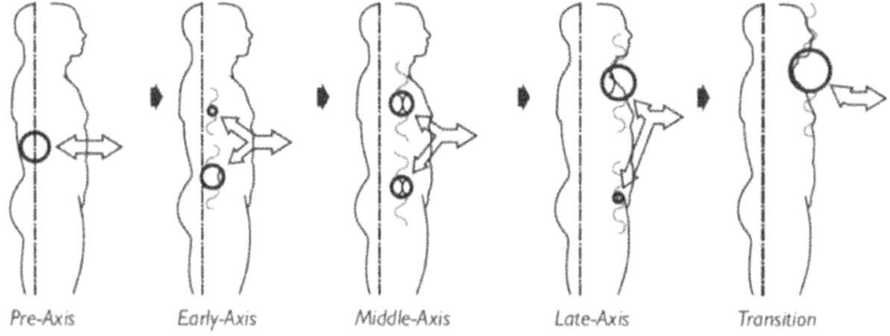

Fig. 4-3. The Evolution of Horizontal and Vertical Polarity[11]

Words and Associations

Understanding that draws on the life of the body in this way takes us beyond how most people think. But it points towards a perspective that should become increasingly important. A more conscious connection with body experiences is one of the gifts that comes with Cultural Maturity's changes. A deeper relationship to body intelligence is key to the way Integrative Meta-perspective provides the complete and systemic understanding needed to progress effectively as a species.

Intelligence's Creative Multiplicity as an Antidote

I promised to return to the assertion that artificial intelligence and human intelligence have little to do with one another. I've gone so far as to propose that the greatest danger in our time may lie with advances in AI running amok. I've also suggested that there may be nothing we can do about it. What I can say comfortably is that, if we are to succeed in escaping this consequence of

---

11   People often responded with confusion when I first referred to "vertical" and "horizontal" dynamics. I responded by being confused that they might be confused. I couldn't think of any way to be more concrete. Inner and Outer seem easiest for people to grasp. Sometimes we experience more from the innermost parts of ourselves; at other times more from the body's surface. In a related way, we encounter more vertical polar dynamics bodily with how one person may seem more Upper, more in his head; while another person acts in ways that are more Lower, more from the gut. To illustrate vertical dynamics when working with a group, I will often line people up from those whose temperaments are most Upper to those whose temperaments are most Lower and then simply walk down the line, pointing my finger at the center of balance of each person's body.

our tool-making prowess, it will happen through a basic understanding of human intelligence and how it is different from what we are calling artificial intelligence.

An appreciation for the fundamental differences is key to understanding not only how such new technology might be effectively managed; but also how overshooting-the-mark Transitional Absurdities might be successfully addressed.

Creative Systems Theory makes the distinction most simply with the recognition that human intelligence reflects the fact that we are living systems. It goes on to propose that the uniquely creative way that human intelligence is structured gives us our remarkable toolmaking, meaning-making prowess. On the other hand, machine intelligence, however amazing and complex, remains machine intelligence. Creative Systems Theory adds detail to these basic observations with the recognition that human intelligence has multiple aspects, each of which organizes experience in a different way.

The theory describes four basic kinds of intelligence that work together to support and drive creative/formative processes. As I address Creative Systems Theory in more detail in the book's Appendix, a basic description here will suffice. We have our rationality, in which we take appropriate pride. But just as important is our emotional intelligence, which gives us feelings and most informs human relationships. There is also imaginal intelligence, that which inspires art and myth. And there is the intelligence of the body, which provides a foundation for all the rest. The Creative Systems Theory notion of Integrative Meta-perspective describes how a newly conscious relationship with intelligence's creative multiplicity is necessary for the kind of understanding that moving forward effectively—and wisely—as a species will require.

To a psychiatrist who spends every day immersed in human intelligence's rich complexities, the differences couldn't be starker and more obvious. And it hasn't escaped people in other fields. Journalist and social scientist David Brooks recently published an article in *The New York Times* titled, "In the Age of A.I., Major in Being Human" (Feb. 2, 2023). Linguist Noam Chomsky recently observed that, "However useful these program may be in narrow domains, we know from the science of linguistics and the philosophy of knowledge that they differ profoundly from the way humans reason and use language. These differences place significant limitations on what the programs can do, encoding them with ineradicable defects." Remarkably, this recognition is not widely shared among people working in the artificial intelligence field.

In my recent book, *Intelligence's Creative Multiplicity: And Its Essential Role in the Future of Understanding*, I suggest that the key to reaping AI's great potential benefits—and avoiding the very real dangers—comes back to a simple question: What can human intelligence do that AI cannot? The same question provides answers to how, more generally, we can get beyond overshooting-the-mark Transitional Absurdities.

Artificial intelligence has parallels with only one aspect of human intelligence: the rational; and, even there, only crude ones. (Our rationality works in ways that are much more nuanced—even mysterious—than we recognize.) This simple recognition gets us a long way to making the needed distinctions between human intelligence and AI. Artificial intelligence is going to do well where rationality in the basic cause-and-effect sense is sufficient. It is even going to do well with complex systemic concerns as long as the systemic relationships are of the mechanistic sort. Indeed, within those parameters it quickly goes beyond anything we could as humans imagine being capable of— and sometimes in ways that can seem quite magical. I think, for example, of the recent recognition that AI could be used to rapidly map the complex folding of hundreds of protein molecules. It can also do things that might look creative, such as writing poetry. Ask Chat GPT to write the last paragraph in the form of a sonnet and it will take but a few seconds to do so. But ultimately it comes up short.

That more is needed is most obviously the case with emotional intelligence, and the tasks of human relationships provide the readiest examples. Anybody who has worked with couples in therapy knows that the rational as often as not gets in the way when it comes to tasks that involve human caring. Those who are not overly adept in ways of the heart could hope that AI might offer a shortcut; but a simple thought experiment quickly dashes that faint hope. Imagine you had the option of acquiring a robot that was programed to be the perfect lover and partner. Would you buy it? (And here I mean not just for fun, but to be your life partner.) And if not, why not?

Within the realm of imaginal intelligence, creativity provides the most immediate reference. Human creativity is not just about being quick or clever. It reaches into the unfathomable and gives expression to what in a moment is just becoming possible. In contrast, even the best "creative" production of AI is derivative. While it might take what exists and arrange it in different, often profoundly complex ways, that is not really creativity. We don't even need to reference formal creativity to confront the essential difference. Think of the creative work of the young child—efforts that come from that period in a life when imaginal intelligence mostly calls the shots. You could easily duplicate it with AI. But what would you have accomplished? And as someone whose background is in art and music, I have yet to see AI-generated art that seemed worthy of my attention. Clever, yes; sometimes even rather remarkable. But cutting and pasting even at the pace possible with a supercomputer is still cutting and pasting. That is not art. I've described how the real thing gives voice to just-emerging capabilities in the human psyche (and with great art, the psyche of culture). Remove the psyche, and you remove significance.

We are not so used to thinking of the body as intelligence; we are more used to thinking of the body in terms of anatomy and physiology. With athletics and sexuality, we at least begin to sense that our bodies are not things we have, but who we are. Creative Systems Theory makes deeper connection with the recognition that body intelligence is where a multitude of formative processes have their beginnings, in faint inklings and rumblings from deep inside us. Our bodies hold our deepest mysteries. They also hold our deepest connections with nature and life as a whole.

The topic that best brings these reflections about intelligence's creative multiplicity together is human purpose. In an important sense, human intelligence is not merely more complex than machine learning in its considerations; it is inherently purposeful. Human intelligence is "designed" to engage us in questions of value and meaning. When I work with a client in therapy, I don't need to direct them toward meaning. In fact, if I did, it would yield the opposite result. I need only engage them deeply in the whole of their internal creative complexity, and purpose follows naturally.

I've described how we confront a Crisis of Purpose and proposed as evidence today's growing prevalence of depression, suicide, degenerative diseases, and gun violence. I've also argued that moving forward effectively—and purposefully—hinges on a next chapter in how we think and act. Cultural Maturity's changes offer that we better understand and more deeply engage the whole of our cognitive complexity. In other words, it requires that we consciously draw on the whole of intelligence's creative multiplicity.

This task is not only about purpose on an individual level, but also about larger human purpose. I've spoken of the importance of redefining progress. Going forward it must be about more than material growth: It must be as much about the health of our human relationships, our capacities for real creativity, our honoring of nature, and our experience of purpose—all things that require that which is unique in human intelligence to engage at all effectively.

The Challenge: I might better have framed the question, "What can human intelligence do—just by its nature—that AI will never be able to do (and how we get ourselves into considerable trouble when we fail to recognize how this is so)?" Some might argue that, given time, AI can address all of these "deficiencies." When seen through the lens of intelligence's creative multiplicity, however, I think the more accurate conclusion is that AI and human intelligence simply don't have a lot to do with each other. Each can serve us, but toward very different ends.

The ultimate task as toolmakers is to know the difference between ourselves and our tools; I think of particular intelligences, like the rational, as tools in this sense. And, however amazing our technologies might be, I certainly think of overshooting-the-mark risks we take with them in a similar way. With Integrative Meta-perspective we can step back and put our achievements in perspective. The hoped-for result is the ability to make wise and compassionate choices going forward.

CHAPTER FIVE

Postmodern Transitional Absurdities

The last kind of Transitional Absurdity perhaps best deserves the name. We encounter it when we succeed at stepping beyond Modern Age beliefs and begin to engage in what I have called Transitional dynamics. We confront it most formally with postmodern thought. But we find it in any situation where we successfully leave behind Modern Age guideposts but have yet to step into Cultural Maturity's more systemic world of experience.

This kind of Transitional Absurdity leaves us stuck in an in-between place between Modern Age cognitive structures and the more complete understanding that manifests with Integrative Meta-perspective. From this place, conclusions fail to manifest what is ultimately needed. And if we don't realize that is the case, we can believe things that are at the least unhelpful; at the most, ludicrous. Sometimes this can be the result simply of Transitional changes pushing us beyond what we can tolerate. But in other instances, it is a product of assuming that Transitional realities themselves represent final truth.

Here I'll start with a general look at postmodern perspective, both its contributions and shortcomings. Next I'll address how contemporary conversations about all kinds of identity—personal, gender, racial— reflect steps forward as well as fail to grasp what is needed. Then I'll examine those identity-related traps that confuse equality and equivalence, and the trap of the angry victim. I'll describe how the postmodern challenge manifests in today's changing relationship to moral/ethical concerns of all sorts. Finally, I'll conclude by introducing a way of thinking about history that looks squarely at the past, warts and all, while avoiding the kind of denigration that too often accompanies postmodern interpretation of history.

Postmodern Thought

Beginning with a description of formal postmodern belief helps put such Transitional thinking in perspective. Postmodern belief had its start in the philosophical ponderings of existentialism. With the growing influence of social constructivism in the later part of the twentieth century, it came to be a central influence in intellectual circles. Postmodern ideas have had major influence in recent decades, particularly in academia. They emphasize our loss of familiar cultural guideposts and "essentialist" truths in general. Advocates of postmodern perspective argue that we "construct" the realities we live in, and they propose that the defining task of the future is to do so more consciously.

While culturally mature perspective views postmodern thought as a useful first step, it emphasizes that surrendering our past cultural absolutes can only be a beginning. We must also learn to relate and think in "post-essentialist" ways—more encompassing, nuanced, complex, and precise. Particularly with the more extreme interpretations, postmodern thought reduces to an unhelpful, one-conclusion-is-as-good-as-another relativism. Overall, postmodern ideas give us at once some of the best and some of the weakest future-related thought.

Coincidentally, formal postmodern/constructivist ideas and Cultural Maturity share several concepts: They both question the absoluteness of past ways of understanding; they emphasize our time's loss of final truths; and they point out that beliefs vary widely between cultures, evolve over time, and are subject to human manipulation. But such thinking fails to help us understand *why* today we see such fundamental questioning of past belief. And of particular importance, rarely does it offer much of real substance to replace what it insightfully recognizes has been taken away.

Formal postmodern/constructivist thought does occasionally make a start toward the needed greater sophistication of understanding. The claim that we "construct" the realities we live in at least implies the possibility of crafting our world in more effective ways. Postmodern/Constructivist thinkers also often make predictions that are generally consistent with more systemically conceived options; for example, how institutions and assumptions of the Modern Age will give way to more fluid and pluralistic cultural structures, and how future understanding will be characterized by multiple perspectives and even contradiction.

But fears of falling back into old absolutes severely limit such thinking, often resulting in Transitional Absurdity. Even the most fully developed postmodern/constructivist ideas stop short of recognizing the kind of cognition changes that getting beyond the limitations of Modern Age belief require. Consequently, they fail to help us "construct" our personal and collective realities in mature—dynamic and complete—ways. They also fail to provide guidance for developing the systemic approaches to understanding that are needed for our future.

Indeed, postmodern/constructivist beliefs often interfere with efforts to go further. Postmodern/constructivist thinkers tend to assume that there are no universal truths; only truths specific to particular times and places. Formal Postmodern/constructivist thinking can get stuck in an immediate skepticism about anything that looks like an overarching concept. This skepticism has admirable roots: Overarching ideas in times past had their origins in narrow and often self-serving beliefs. But postmodern thought's common distaste for big-picture conception—indeed conception of any substantive sort— undercuts its ability to contribute creatively to the larger conversation.

Postmodern theorists tend to be better at critique than they are at providing useful perspective. And often theirs is a most limited—indeed, limiting and deadening—kind of critique. Identification with our inability to know with certainty, and with our different-strokes-for-different-folks notions of diversity, ultimately undermines efforts to effectively move forward.

Over the last couple of decades, Postmodern/Constructivist sensibility has come simultaneously to lose its hold in academic circles and gain a growing influence in spheres of popular expression. In contemporary art, music, humor, and popular culture, we see increased use of irony and a mixing of influences, often from far-flung sources. As with the earlier, more formal postmodern contribution, this popular influence has at once invited the beginnings of more complex and multifaceted sensibility but resulted in efforts that contribute much less than they claim. Too often we find popular expressions that confuse the glib, ironic, and simply random with substance. All too often it translates into a difference-for-its-own-sake cleverness that says very little while pretending to be profound.

Digital media has played a major role in amplifying postmodern sensibility's influence. Again, we see both benefits and dangers. Digital media's ability to link massive amounts of information with people of vastly differing backgrounds and beliefs fosters diversity of perspective. At the same time, it has played into postmodern sensibility's tendency to confuse random associations and undifferentiated stimulation with significance.

In the previous chapter, I noted how digital media contributes to Transitional Absurdities of the surface stimulation sort. Certainly we see this with social media. While it claims to be about connectedness, social media often leaves us estranged in a world of superficial, largely random, and self-centered associations. While it can provide social connections, it also contributes to a world in which we commonly confuse the most trivial of human contact with real relationships. If postmodern sensibility did not so define meaning in our times, we would find this situation quite ludicrous.

We also find such postmodern absurdity in the proliferation of digital content that claims to be serious; for example, what has come to constitute news in an on-line world. News that is selected for us based on algorithms that assume what we want to see (such as Google News) end up combining significance randomly with the worst of triviality (real news and celebrity gossip get equal billing). And the most superficial of digital "news" is little more than clickbait masquerading as meaning. While on-line news coverage that is curated by traditional news sources can be something of an exception, even here we are not spared from Transitional Absurdity. At the same time that news should be providing systemic perspective, we tend increasingly to find predictable political/social biases—think Fox News on the Right and NPR and the *New York Times* on the Left. Sadly, I know of no news source that reliably provides culturally mature content.

The postmodern/constructivist contribution, whether formal or popular, reflects well the unsettling realities of our transitional age. When timely, it helps us get beyond the past's heroic/romantic assumptions, challenges ideology, and confronts worlds that seem contradictory only from the perspective of that which we have known. But in the end, a postmodern worldview fails to grasp what, if anything, lies beyond today's loss of familiar truths. Because of this, it fails to provide a useful guiding story for the future. When this failure is extreme, sensibility becomes, in effect, Transitional Absurdity.

Postmodern Realities and Identity

Some of the most consequential postmodern challenges concern identity. Here I include individual identity—how we think about what identity means to a person. I also include more collective forms of identity, such as how we think about gender, or about ethnicity and race. Because today's identity-related changes are so fundamental, they can easily overwhelm us. Particularly during awkward, in-between times when changes are taking place, we can reach conclusions that are best thought of as Transitional Absurdity.

Part of what is becoming different about identity is simply a result of the loss of traditional guideposts. But identity's new picture is also a product of the ways both identity and human relationship begin to change as we approach Cultural Maturity's threshold. In times past, both identity and relationship were based on projection—attributing aspects of ourselves to others. With Cultural Maturity, the realities of both identity and relationship become more of a Whole-Person sort.

To understand how our thinking about identity—and how identity itself—is changing, it helps to look at the last time history witnessed this kind of shift. Starting some five hundred years ago, Europe's new Modern Age gave us our now familiar concept of the individual. With the art of the Renaissance, for the first time, figures depicted were not just symbols, but mortals; and works of art were signed, marked as the achievements of particular people. Later, in the world of love, with the advent of the modern romantic ideal, the bonds between men and women became the providence of individual inclinations. Over time, a more individualistic picture of identity transformed institutions of all sorts, giving us the Reformation's newly personal relationship to God, institutional democracy (with determination now a product of the votes of individuals), capitalist economic systems (based on competition between individuals), and modern higher education (increasingly a vehicle to prepare people for this degree of individual choice). These changes could not have been more significant.

But there is no reason to assume that the Modern Age's picture of identity—in which we have taken appropriate pride—represents some last word. Creative Systems Theory makes clear that it can't be. The concept of Cultural Maturity predicts that further chapters in identity's evolutionary story lie ahead. It also makes clear that, if our thinking about identity stops where we are today, we will have major problems. The following radical observation both supports these conclusions and points toward what more is needed: The Modern Age concept of the individual was in fact not about individuality at all. Modern Age changes brought greater autonomy, certainly; but they left us short of individual identity in any complete sense.

Creative Systems Theory calls this misconception—that the Modern Age concept has fully defined our identity—the Myth of the Individual. To illustrate why it is a myth we need only consider the future of love, leadership, and broad social relationships, such as those we frame in the language of race. In each case, over recent centuries we celebrated a new realization of the individual. A world in which love was determined by family or a matchmaker, along with authoritarian forms of leadership, gave way to experiencing choice as ours to make. Similarly, recent liberation movements have made ethnic and racial equality a legitimate consideration. Key to what made each of these new realizations a reality was a greater perceived role for the individual.

However, in each case, the belief that we had fully become individuals was illusionary because, in each case, identity was based on projection. Modern Age romantic love relied on finding one's "brave knight" or "fair maiden," a mythic "other half" that would be our completion. Under Modern Age leadership we still projected authority onto presidents, professors, and doctors, making them greater than ordinary people. And regarding ethnicity and race, bigotry remained. Even when identity was strong and positive, it tended to be framed in terms of oppressor and oppressed. Each kind of identity was set in the context of what Creative Systems Theory calls "two-halves-make-a-whole" relationship, where each person represents half of a larger systemic entirety. Being half of a systemic whole is not about being an individual—certainly not in any fully realized sense.

Today, love, leadership, and broader social identities require that we relate in more complete, more Whole-Person/Whole-System ways. The critical implication is that a Whole-Person relationship is about a new, more complete kind of relationship with ourselves. It requires that we reincorporate projections, step back, and more fully engage all of who we are. With Cultural Maturity's changes, being an individual takes on a fundamentally different meaning: Individual identity becomes about consciously holding the whole of our human complexity.

What at first might seem a contradiction provides both evidence for Whole-Person identity's newness and additional feedback for recognizing its achievement. Whole-Person "individuality" makes us fully different and thus more authentically individual. At the same time, it makes us more capable of deep and authentic relationships.

Whole-Person relationship requires that we leave behind our past mythologized—and thus dependent—relationship with the other. In doing so, for the first time we are able to stand fully separate. We also engage ourselves in more complete ways, and in so doing embrace all that makes us uniquely who we are. With Whole-Person relationship—and identity—we step beyond an illusionary separateness, and in its place experience our authentic difference.

Concurrently, we witness a deepened capacity for connectedness. Whole-Person love offers the possibility of more complete and enduring love. In a similar way, Whole-Person/Whole-System leadership offers deeper and more authentic engagement between leaders and those the leader represents. Likewise we find a growing capacity for mutual appreciation of social identities such as ethnicity and race. This deeper connectedness is a product of the simple fact that we now bring the whole of ourselves to the task of relating and are thus capable of engaging in fuller ways. But Integrative Meta-perspective makes a further kind of contribution: It makes it possible for us to draw more consciously on parts of ourselves that appreciate that to live is to be connected—and not only with particular individuals, but also with community, nature, and existence in general.

Since the Myth of the Individual can seem startling on first encounter, I will quickly sum up its concept and implications. In times past, we imagined ourselves to be distinct and complete, when in reality we were identifying with half of larger systemic wholes. In this sense, we were in fact not really separate.

In contrast, Whole-Person identity allows us to stand truly separate for the first time. In doing so, we become capable of a new depth of connectedness to ourselves and a fuller appreciation for what makes who we are unique. At the same time, because Whole-Person identity makes it possible to engage others from the whole of who we are, we become capable of a depth of relationship that has not before been an option. And because the cognitive changes we need for such relating help us draw on aspects of ourselves that support connectedness, the possibility of deep and complex bonds is further enhanced.

The Myth of the Individual and Transitional Absurdity

The kinds of changes that expose the Myth of the Individual and offer the possibility of more Whole-Person identity and relationship begin to manifest with Transition. But it is also the case that the dynamics of Transition can leave us in an in-between place during their realization. A variety of predictable Transitional Absurdities result.

With regard to identity, the most obvious is that we can be left hanging precariously between definitions. The Modern Age image of the individual as an ideal and an end-point fails us; but at the same time, we have nothing to replace it with. The fact that Transition leaves us alienated from our bodies, disconnected from nature, and without any real depth of connection in community, makes the situation even more precarious.

Regarding love and human relationships in general, we find ourselves without the mythologizing that in times past provided the glue of relationship. The easy magnetisms of "two-halves-make-a-whole" connections abandon us; and, limited to the postmodern realities of transition, this can feel like the end of things. I suspect that such dynamics today play a major role in escalating divorce rates and the difficulties so many people experience in relationships. In working with couples in therapy, I often find such awkward, in-between dynamics underlying confusions and conflicts.

I think of this dynamic as forming the basis for much of today's crisis of confidence in leadership. In part, the fact that we are tending to refrain from mythologizing leaders, elevating them and putting them on pedestals is a good thing. But without something to replace such mythologizing, it becomes very difficult for leadership to function. We end up with anti-authoritarian beliefs and a general lack of trust in institutions, undermining any possibility of effective decision making.

Regarding broader social identities, we find ourselves in the throes of modern identity politics. On the one hand we find greater acceptance of equal rights and equal opportunity. But while overt bigotry becomes less and less acceptable, covert forms of bigotry remain. And people find it very difficult to talk about ethnicity or race in any other language than that of oppression. This awkward, in-between place makes it hard to experience ethnic or racial identities separate from the perceived "other." It also creates a situation in which steps that take us closer to mutual understanding often exacerbate ethnic and racial tensions.

Rethinking Gender Identity

This brings us to the problem of stopping postmodern Transitional pictures of identity and relationship, and how that produces predictable traps and distortions. Transitional dynamics bring with them foreseeable ideological beliefs and conceptual traps in the areas of identity and relationships. A good place to see such traps is in the ways we can get intractably stuck in today's conversations about gender.

A look at how Creative Systems Theory frames current changes reshaping our relationship to gender provides a good way in. The theory points toward two kinds of changes that are key to today's evolving gender realities. The first brings us back to the recognition that psychological qualities can be thought of as archetypally masculine, others archetypally feminine: We experience them as harder or softer, more expressive or more receptive. Historically, the theory proposes, we have never understood gender just for what it is. Rather, when we looked at someone of the "opposite sex," what we saw was projected gender archetypes. It was this that gave us the traditional picture, with two wholly-distinct gender categories. The theory delineates how the differing ways gender differences have been perceived at different periods in culture reflect how the relationship between archetypally masculine and archetypally feminine qualities has manifested at particular times and places.

The first kind of change is a result of appreciating how everyone manifests both archetypally masculine and archetypally feminine qualities. The Creative Systems Theory concept of Cultural Maturity highlights the mechanism of such change. It describes how it is becoming possible in our time to step back and consciously engage the whole of ourselves—the whole of our human complexity. Archetypally masculine and archetypally feminine reflect two key aspects of that complexity. With Cultural Maturity's changes we are better able to "bridge" the masculine and feminine in ourselves and in a similar way to understand others with a newly systemic kind of completeness. We see how, in an important sense, we are all "non-binary."

This first kind of change, while profound, represents only a start. It takes us beyond the historical rigidity of gender roles and gender-specific notions of identity; but more is needed. It is too easy to confuse embracing the whole of our complexity simply with the freedom to choose our gender. We end up in a unisex world; or, alternatively, a world with an infinity of options, none more appropriate than another. Today we reside in an awkward, in-between time with regard to gender-related changes.

The second kind of change takes us the rest of the way, although its recognition is almost wholly missing in today's gender conversation. Cultural Maturity's changes not only "bridge" archetypally masculine and archetypally feminine, but they also accomplish the same with the polarity of mind and body. This further kind of change has major consequences for the gender conversation. It helps us more deeply engage ourselves as gendered beings. In a culturally mature reality, while it is true that psychologically everyone is non-binary, we also come to live more deeply and more fully in our bodies—including our sexuality, however it might manifest.

When we combine these two kinds of change, we get a picture that takes the gender conversation forward in ways that are once freeing and grounding. The combination encourages a more fluid and complex relationship to gender and gender roles, one with many more options. And at the same time it invites a person to celebrate being a man or a woman, whatever the particular balance of qualities that comes with that person's temperament, and whatever that person's sexual orientation.

Common Traps

When we stop halfway in this two-part process, we leave ourselves vulnerable to traps in our thinking, a couple of which have particular consequences. We encounter each of these with contemporary identity politics, whether the politics of gender identity or those of ethnic and racial identity. In the first, we confuse equity with equivalence. In the second, we get caught in victim narratives that ultimately undermine real empowerment.

Confusing equality and equivalence

Postmodern advocacy tends to make the ultimate goal equality, and stop there. In contrast, culturally mature perspective is careful not to confuse equality with equivalence. When it comes to gender, Creative Systems Theory brings nuance to this difference.

With the recognition that both men and women embody archetypally masculine and feminine characteristics, the theory's systemic picture further affirms that men and women are more similar than we have assumed in times past. But it also helps us better appreciate normative differences. Today the suggestion that we might find differences of any kind between men and women can be controversial. Contemporary academic thought may claim that psychological differences, if they exist at all, are products of conditioning, of the different ways that boys and girls are raised. Indeed, it is possible in academia today to lose one's job simply for suggesting the existence of differences of a more fundamental sort. But that there are real differences seems obvious to most people. Very few individuals who spend much time with young children, for example, would agree that their upbringing is enough to explain gender differences.

How *are* men and women in fact different—if they are at all? At the very least, we live in different kinds of bodies. Given how both Modern Age thought and the different-strokes-for-different-folks assumptions of postmodern belief each point toward what is, in effect, a disembodied future; the fact that we have different kinds of bodies might seem of minor significance. But this can't be our direction going forward. A key characteristic of Cultural Maturity's changes is that they help us get more in touch with the body as experience.

We gain important further insight by turning to observations about the relative balance of psychological characteristics. While here we are necessarily dealing with generalities, they prove useful. Once we leave behind polarized expectations, along with finding greater individual variation, we also better recognize normative differences. Men on average tend to embody a bit more of the archetypally masculine; women tend on average to embody somewhat more of the archetypally feminine. I think of about a 60/40 ratio of archetypal qualities relative to gender.

Body dynamics support this conclusion. Note that men tend to carry their center of balance somewhat higher in the body, in the chest and shoulders, and women somewhat lower, in the pelvis and thighs. And even with the same amount of exertion and conditioning, men's bodies tend to be a bit harder to the touch and women's a bit softer. A person could dismiss these observations as "just physical." But, as CST makes clear, the notion that anything is merely physical is more a product of our time in culture than how things actually work. Reflection on personality style differences in Chapter Six will expand on this kind of observation.

Such recognition of normative differences requires that we think in ways that we may not be used to, but it can be powerfully freeing. Simultaneously, it takes us beyond history's polarized expectations and unisex notions that in their own ways can be just as constraining. Suddenly our gender options multiply. And our task in relationship to gender becomes newly clear and obvious: simply to be as fully ourselves as we are able.

This more systemic way of thinking about gender differences will for many people lessen the controversy; but given that conflict in belief often tends to be a product of ideology, we should not expect to get rid of controversy entirely. And implications regarding more specific gender-related questions can arouse intense feelings even among those who might not have any difficulty with the basic picture that I've described.

Current debates about equality in the workplace provide a good example. Equal opportunity and equal pay for equal work are unquestionable goods. But if we find gender differences in the number of people in particular professions, it's implied that the only legitimate explanation is discrimination. Very often, discrimination is indeed the major factor. But the recognition of normative differences also suggests other possibilities. What we are most attracted to, for example, could also play a role. Some jobs are more appealing to those with more of the archetypally masculine in their makeup, others to those who most manifest the archetypally feminine. That will be the case for both men and women; but if the idea of a 60/40 normative balance is accurate, there are going to be normative differences too in the jobs men and women are drawn to. Fifty years from now, differences should be less extreme than what we see today, and certainly much less extreme than those we have seen historically. But even if discrimination with regard to job opportunity is totally eliminated, in most professions discrepancies will likely remain. I suspect we will still see more male firefighters and race car drivers than women; and more women nurses and teachers of young children.

We find the distinction between equality and equivalence important anywhere we encounter bigotry. Bigotry is a statement about difference; but this is difference based on projection, and thus ultimately on two-halves-make-a-whole relationships with their lack of authentic difference. Getting beyond bigotry involves better recognizing our commonality, but that is just a start if our interest is not merely liberal niceness but also seeing things in ways that increase possibility. A culturally mature transcendence of bigotry also necessarily involves appreciating that we may authentically differ in many ways, including in our historical experiences. It may involve different shared values. And it involves the willingness to entertain even deeper sorts of differences. In my book *The Creative Systems Personality Typology*, I observe that certain personality styles are found more often than the norm in people of particular ethnic or racial backgrounds. In today's world, suggesting differences of any kind between homogeneous groups is controversial. But I also note important implications not just for better getting along, but also for making our institutions work for everyone equally.

I've described how culturally mature perspective challenges ideological correctness of both the political left and the political right. The above reflections on differentiating equality and equivalence provide good illustration. Liberals are likely to bristle at any suggestion that differences are not simply a product of discrimination. We find this with the simple-mindedness of extreme populist, "woke" advocacy. Conservatives are more likely to feel there is something sacred in traditional assumptions. We see this with the equally simple-minded reactive conclusions of contemporary far-right populism. Framing what we see in terms of how we understand, and the evolution of understanding, offers the possibility of a more complete kind of relationship to our own identity as well as to the identities of others.

The Trap of the Victim Narrative

It is important to recognize that the word "identity" as used in the phrase "identity politics" most often stops well short of the complete sort of identity that comes with Integrative Meta-perspective. This could seem to be only an issue of semantics; but one consequence of this difference is that, while contemporary identity politics tends to be associated with progress, advancement is often less frequent than advocates like to assume.

An increasingly prevalent and dangerous consequence of identity politics helps clarify why this is predictable. Identity politics tends to define identity in "victim" terms. Too often we find ourselves in a reality of competing victim narratives, in which we assume that whichever person or group feels most mistreated and misjudged wins. In the end, it is a competition in which no one is the victor. Victim narratives distort our thinking and make it impossible for anyone to effectively move forward. In the end, they reflect but the other side of the coin to the dominance narratives of times past.

Victim narratives increasingly define identity on both the political right and the political left. This is particularly the case at ideology's populist extremes. From the populist Right we hear victim narratives described in response to college-educated coastal elites, critical race theory, and government encroachment on individual freedoms with vaccine mandates. Victim narratives from the populist Left are framed in the language of patriarchy, racism of an all-encompassing systemic sort, gender discrimination, and white privilege. In each case, people end up defining legitimacy in terms of how many injustice boxes are checked.

Perceived historical injustices and inequalities are often very real—and not infrequently horrendously so. And we gain much by seeing history clearly, including its very significant warts and often glaring time-specific transgressions. But while the ability to do so reflects an important kind of advancement in our time, defining oneself as a victim is different. When we stop at the language of trauma and victimization, not only do we once again end up thinking simplistically about complex dynamics; but we also end up responding in ways that get in the way of moving forward.

Psychologically, victim narratives—and particularly today's idealization of the angry victim—are in the end little different from the stories we've told in times past to justify bigotry and war. We make another the symbolic cause of our pain. We focus on grievances and attribute what we feel to some "evil other." The price we pay goes well beyond just simple-minded conclusions and historical distortions: We make culturally mature conversation essentially impossible.

Most immediately, because victim narratives create worlds of us-versus-them instead of supporting mutual understanding, they produce thinking that sets us even further apart. As any good psychologist knows, people who see the world in victim terms tend to be some of the quickest to victimize. At the least they are just as vulnerable as an oppressor to failing to find humanity in the other. We have seen even further growing apart over recent decades wherever identity politics has come to define debate.

If one's concern is real change, of even greater importance is that victim narratives are ultimately disempowering—and in a particularly insidious way. When we place all responsibility outside ourselves, we also put authority outside ourselves. We blind ourselves not only to the complexity of perspective needed to effectively make changes; but also to the necessary agency and initiative required to effect the kind of change that we most hope to foster.

The assumptions of identity politics almost always capture important aspects of larger truths. And sometimes such advocacy can provide limited benefit, at least in the short term. But identity politics ultimately tends to be more about feeling secure in one's ideological superiority and cementing bonds of allegiance than it is about the maturity of perspective on which essential change depends. Even when it has its roots in legitimate observations and commendable impulses, identity defined in this way tends to get in the way of where we need to go. We need to do better if our efforts are to be effective.

In the next chapter, I will describe a "hands-on" approach that directly supports the realization of culturally mature understanding. In it, a person addresses their different parts as if they are characters in a play. With culturally mature understanding, the person is in charge, and parts function like consultants. When we stop short, however, parts take over and run the show. Victim narratives can provide a step forward in the sense that they challenge oppression—and often a debilitating history of oppression. But this challenge comes only from one part. Because of this, the victim narrative not only fails to provide identity in any complete sense: It can get in the way of understanding what a fully-empowered identity might look like.

Nobel laureate and Pulitzer Prize winning author Toni Morrison offered a good way to think about the needed completeness of identity, from the side of those who have been oppressed. She first referenced James Baldwin's observation that black writers tend to write as if they have a white man on their shoulder that they need to convince. She then described how she tried to write "without the white gaze." I think the fact that she succeeded was a major part of what made her writing so effective. While the white inner-critic has origins in real oppression, today it exists as an unhelpful internal part. One essential implication is that, while oppression as it currently exists needs to be addressed; at a certain point, change on the part of the perceived oppressor is limited in relieving one from feeling oppressed. That feat requires re-owning projections and learning to live "without the white gaze."

Addressing issues of equality and oppression requires everyone involved to engage identity more systemically. That includes people who have been oppressed no longer claiming superiority by projecting unsavory aspects of their makeup onto others. It also entails that people who have been oppressed not project their own authority—and with this the place within themselves from which they judge worth and identity—onto others; to ensure they are not giving away the power to affirm that indeed they matter.

The Postmodern Moral Quandary

Looking at effectively addressing moral questions today summarizes the postmodern dilemma and clarifies what getting beyond it will ask of us. The moral dimension today presents a startling and unsettling circumstance. Effectively addressing moral challenges requires new human capacities: ones that previously we could not have fully understood, much less applied. In part this is because we confront new kinds of moral questions; for example, those that follow from the need to manage the often two-edged implications of new technologies and the frequently confusing and overwhelming complexities of our increasingly globalized world. But the reason is ultimately deeper. What moral questions of every sort are asking of us is changing, and these changes affect what it means to make good decisions in every part of our lives.

Most people today think about morally-charged concerns quite differently than they did but a few decades ago. It is essential that we understand exactly what is changing and why. Not everyone finds these changes positive, and even those people who see them as good can find them confusing and overwhelming. The concept of Cultural Maturity describes how what we see is predicted and how it represents only a beginning. It goes on to argue that our understanding of needed new moral capacities and learning to put them into practice will be key to a healthy human future.

In thinking about what is becoming different, I find it helpful to conceptualize a couple of steps—ones that should now begin to feel familiar. The first step immediately throws us into Transitional realities. It turns our attention to today's marked weakening of traditional moral guideposts. Historically, culture provided us with reliable moral absolutes. Today the sources of clear guidance, from unquestioned national and ethnic allegiances to once-and-for-all religious beliefs, are losing their power.

Given the significance of this weakening of absolutes, it is important that we understand why we are seeing it. Contrasting interpretations can get highly charged: People of a conservative bent tend to view it negatively, as a loss of social order; or worse, as a sign of impending moral chaos. On the other hand, liberal types are apt to think of it positively, as an expression of new freedom, evidence of liberation from constraining rules. And academics tend to view today's loss of past cultural guideposts more neutrally, as a reflection of a new postmodern cultural narrative.

However, as we interpret such changing moral realities, we find ourselves in the awkward, in-between circumstance. With nothing of substance to replace what has been taken away, we can feel adrift. At best, we are left with an empty moral relativism. We get different-strokes-for-different-folks thinking, which leaves us wandering aimlessly in an increasingly complex moral landscape. This circumstance reaches an absurd extreme today as "likes" and "clicks" increasingly become our modern measures of significance.

In important ways, this in-between place takes us forward; but it necessarily remains short of what we need in order to make effective moral decisions. We see both personal and collective moral challenges. The sexual revolution of the last century is a good example of a personal challenge: While it freed people from the limiting constraints of times past, it presented choices that they often later regretted. Effective moral decision-making has to be about more than just "anything goes" freedom; it must somehow provide a deeper basis for making moral determinations.

This awkward in-between place in the moral arena is also apparent when intractable moral quandaries leave social groups at odds. Earlier I used the abortion debate to illustrate the challenge of addressing polarization. It also provides insight for the more general task of bringing culturally mature perspective to the moral sphere. I am comfortable asserting that the legalizing of abortion was an important step forward. But framing the abortion question simply in terms of "abortion rights" oversimplifies an immensely complex moral concern. It should not be surprising that the question of abortion leaves not just particular groups at odds, but whole nations divided.

The first new ingredient is this Transitional circumstance. The second turns to the new moral capacities that addressing today's moral challenges require of us. If we are to assume the greater responsibility required when we leave behind a parental mythologizing of truth, and we step beyond the postmodern conundrum, we need to think and act in new ways. This need for new moral capacities further contributes to Transitional Absurdity in that these new capacities stretch us. What they ask easily takes us beyond what we can readily tolerate; but if the concept of Cultural Maturity is correct, they also provide the needed guidance for going forward.

Below I've described four such needed new capacities. Each involves stepping beyond past moral absolutes and learning to think in ways that directly approach that which makes an act or thought moral. Each follows naturally from Cultural Maturity's changes and the more whole-box-of crayons understanding that results. Each also involves addressing moral questions in more encompassing ways.

Getting beyond moral polarization—the fact of "competing goods"

We tend to assume that moral quandaries require us to distinguish right from wrong. In fact, this is rarely the case; rather they challenge us to choose in the face of competing goods. When a decision can be reduced to right versus wrong, we are unlikely to experience it as a quandary. The best choice will seem self-evident (most people won't recognize that anything needs deciding).

The abortion debate again provides a good illustration. While it tends to reduce quickly to shrill advocacy, it is very much about competing goods—the sanctity of life on one hand and the choice of the mother on the other. Immigration, another quandary that I touched on as an example in Chapter Two, similarly juxtaposes commendable values; and, in each case, values that we can think of as moral. It is true that immigration responds to needs that any compassionate person should feel moved by. It has also historically supported vibrant societies. But it is also correct that people who have worked—perhaps for generations—to create institutions and economies should not be forced to make the rewards of those efforts freely available to anyone who might desire them (boundaries have a legitimate function).

In suggesting that we need to get beyond framing moral distinctions in polarized, good-versus-evil terms, I am not at all arguing against taking strong moral stands; in fact, Cultural Maturity specifically encourages and supports us in doing so. Engaging moral questions systemically provides the perspective needed to take moral stands confidently and in ways that will support the greatest good.

Recognizing how questions of all sorts are ultimately moral concerns

In a different way, the second new capacity reflects the importance of more encompassing perspective. In times past, only certain kinds of concerns were considered moral issues. Culturally mature perspective's more systemic vantage helps us appreciate how questions of all sorts have value, and thus imply morality.

This change affects not only personal moral choices, but also moral concerns we must address together. We recognize, for example, how domains we've always thought of as "value free"—such as business and science—

represent values just as much as the domains of religion and politics, where choices are obviously value-laden. With Wall Street's role in the financial collapse of 2007, we were confronted with the urgency of recognizing—and questioning when necessary—values that have been common in business. Applying this lesson to our scientific endeavors, we appreciate that future human well-being will depend as much on the maturity needed to use invention wisely as it will be on the particulars of what we might invent.

We can think of the topic that I used to conclude Chapter Two as an ultimate collective moral concern. Rethinking wealth and progress challenges us to collectively ask what ultimately matters, and to use our answer to shape our future.

Learning to think directly in terms of whether a thought or act is "life-enhancing"

The third new capacity is implied in each of the first two. Without culturally specific guideposts, we need to address moral questions more directly. Today we are becoming responsible not just for making necessary decisions, but for reaching deeply into ourselves to determine exactly what we should base our choices on. If our choices are to reflect anything more than postmodern "anything goes" thinking, this is something we must learn how to do.

This observation leaves us with another essential question: If the task is not to choose right over wrong (as I suggested earlier, in emphasizing the fact of competing goods), just what is it? What is the distinction we want to make?

Culturally mature perspective suggests that we ultimately want to determine the degree to which an act enhances life. This conclusion requires that we expand the way we customarily use language (for example, how we relate to life's opposite—death). In the end, however, the degree to which an act is life-enhancing is what moral truth has always been about. Culturally-specific moral dictates have provided shared, one-size-fits-all shorthand for this kind of determination.

With Cultural Maturity's changes, it becomes increasingly possible to set shorthand aside, as culturally mature perspective lets us think more directly in terms of what makes an act moral. We then become better able to take into account all that is involved and to articulate where our considerations take us, in "whole-ball-of-wax" terms.

A few examples that draw from reflections made earlier in the chapter highlight places where this more complete kind of determination is becoming pertinent: While a rewarding life as a man or woman today requires a willingness to question past gender dictates, this is necessarily but a first step. Each of us also needs to more deeply engage the whole of who we are—our full complexity as gendered beings. Similarly, success in love has come to require more than confronting past assumptions and allowing for new options. It also demands a new and deeper appreciation for the needs that love fulfills— companionship, intimate bonds, parental cooperation, and so on. In a related way, a fulfilling sense of identity requires that we go beyond questioning past cultural expectations. In addition, we must draw on a more personal and complete relationship to the question of what creates worth for us.

With each of these examples the task is the same. We need, first, to be attentive to all the factors that may be pertinent. Then, from this more encompassing vantage, we need to take our best shot at choosing the most life-enhancing way forward. Cultural Maturity's cognitive changes make it newly possible to engage in this kind of determination, at once more personal and more sophisticated.

We can again turn to that collective moral truth responsibility, rethinking wealth and progress. When we include everything we need to include, we are asking what kind of choices going forward will be most ultimately life-affirming.

Recognizing that moral choice always happens in a context

Our fourth kind of new capacity even more explicitly takes us beyond postmodern arbitrariness. I've noted how moral relativity of the postmodern, "anything goes" sort is a dangerous trap. In contrast, according to culturally mature perspective, the recognition that good moral choices are alway context-dependent becomes central. This is a new kind of recognition, one that requires Cultural Maturity's changes to fully appreciate and put into practice.

Moral dictates of times past not only were considered eternal, once-and-for-all; they were also thought to apply in exactly the same way to everyone. Culturally mature perspective helps us appreciate that what makes an act life-affirming may be very different, depending on its time and place. It also makes possible specific tools for making needed, more context-specific distinctions.

The Golden Rule, "Do unto others as you would have them do unto you," is a remarkably reliable guide for making moral choices. But when we step over Cultural Maturity's threshold, we are quickly confronted with the Golden Rule's dependence on context. Different people want different things "done unto them" as a function of many factors, including cultural stage, upbringing, and personality style.

Some of morality's relativities are temporal; that is, what is most life-enhancing is dependent on time, particularly developmental time. For example, we have different expectations of a child than we have of an adolescent; and different of an adolescent than that of an adult. If we fail to observe these differences, we can easily act in ways that violate those we most care about. This same kind of temporal relativity plays out culturally. Thus, if we are to fully appreciate why a Muslim woman might find it preferable to wear the hijab, we need to understand cultural stage differences.

Making sense of the moral implications of cultural stage differences is becoming increasingly critical when it comes to questions of global policy. Certainly we need to better appreciate how different kinds of governance work best at different cultural stages. Otherwise, dangerously misguided actions will result—as witnessed by the well-intended but premature attempts by the West to promote Western-style democratic rule following the Arab Spring in the Middle East.

Other aspects of morality's relativity are of a more here-and-now sort. I'm particularly aware of how this kind of contextual relativity plays out with temperaments across personality style differences. The Creative Systems Personality Typology describes the profoundly different ways the world looks through the eyes of people with contrasting personality styles.

As a therapist, in working with couples I've been struck by the frequency with which people with very different temperaments become partners. (We've always recognized that opposites attract; but in the past, this was usually limited to opposites within the same general personality type.) Such "mixed-type" connecting reflects Cultural Maturity's changes and can work out great. But it works only to the degree that differences in what people like "done unto them" are understood and respected. In my work as a consultant to organizations, I see a similar new recognition of the value in bringing a diversity of people on board—another expected result of Cultural Maturity's changes. But again, diversity can serve us only if it is understood and differences honored.

The future is demanding—and making possible—a new kind of moral maturity. It requires taking greater personal and collective responsibility in our choices. It also requires engaging more directly in what makes a choice moral, and applying new conceptual tools that help us make needed, more nuanced distinctions. All these things become possible with Cultural Maturity's cognitive changes and the resulting systemic view of the world.

There is a way in which this new moral reality makes moral choices more straightforward, if not simpler. The same detailed knowledge of culture-specific social mores is not so necessary. And at the same time, the moral challenge becomes much greater. The needed new capacities demand that we hold reality in ways that stretch us in ways that are more inclusive and complete. And the distinctions that Cultural Maturity's changes make possible demand a level of sophistication that would not have made sense to us before now.

Stuck in the middle of these changes, we can easily feel disoriented, as if something has gone terribly wrong. We can think of this feeling in itself as a kind of Transitional Absurdity. Certainly it can lead to confusion, anxiety, and despondency. We also find Transitional Absurdity when the lack of familiar moral guideposts lead to decisions that do not serve us. And no other change in our times is more likely to overwhelm us and lead to regressive responses than the need to add this new responsibility to our moral choices, and the new moral capacities that doing so effectively requires.

A Critique of the Postmodern Critique of Religion

The postmodern critique of religion provides a good example of how getting stuck halfway leaves us short. It is not surprising given how Transition disconnects from connectedness, that postmodern types tend to be critical of religion. We see this from the claims of early existentialists such as Nietzsche that that "God is dead," to the more contemporary thinkers such as Richard Dawkins and Michael Dennett who have become celebrities by virtue of their atheistic claims.

While the concept of Cultural Maturity challenges the mythologized beliefs of traditional religion, it ends up in a very different place than the invalidation of all religion. Indeed, it suggests that atheism is itself perhaps best thought of as a form of fundamentalist religion.

I am comfortable making the perhaps surprising assertion that the "Is God real?" question is not that useful. A person might assume that my reason for this conclusion is the one commonly put forward by self-described atheists, namely that efforts to rationally prove the existence of God through history have never succeeded. But while I would generally agree with this observation, my reason for setting the question aside could just as well be thought of as coming down on the opposite side of the argument. It has more to do with the poverty of atheism as a concept. While the religion versus atheism debate certainly sells books, I find atheism as a belief a bit silly. The vehemence we commonly find with its adherents suggests that it is best thought of as but another form of fundamentalism. More specifically, in leaving out the evolutionary dimension of understanding, the argument for atheism doesn't hold up.

If I argued that the ancient Greeks were wrong for believing there were gods atop Olympus, or that tribal societies have been wrong for having animistic deities, you would appropriately conclude that I had missed the point. While these kinds of beliefs may not be workable today, in their time they gave expression to an important need; and more deeply, I would argue, reflected an essential aspect of human sensibility. I agree, as the advocate for atheism may be quick to point out, that the more modern idea of a monotheistic God with a capital "G" has resulted in harm as well as benefit. But as I see things, the larger portion of that harm, while it may have been in the name of religion, has come not from religion per se, but from our systemic need for worlds of "us and them." And while it is true, too, that religion makes little sense rationally and can lead to some claims that don't hold up, that is not what is important. Religion through time has given expression to essential aspects of being human, aspects that are just as important in our time, and arguably now more important than ever.

From the perspective of Cultural Maturity, religion as we have known it in the Modern Age is best thought of not in terms of the rightness or wrongness of its assertions, but as one chapter in an evolving picture of truth. The important question becomes what a next chapter might look like.

A related issue is how postmodern thinkers have challenged the modern denial of death. In this they have made an important contribution. But again,

Transitional dynamics can leave this critique's outcome wanting. It is not that they fail to entertain the prospect of anything being possible after death, although some dismiss such options along with religion. Cultural Maturity perspective is comfortable with the conclusion that we can't really know. For this reason, this conclusion can often be seen as a reason for despair, the ultimate "existential crisis." Ergo, postmodern thinkers are often depicted as a rather dour lot. Certainly, the view that Transitional dynamics are the end point is not hopeful. In the popular sphere, we end up with the modern prevalence of dystopian narratives.

Creative Systems Theory describes how the sensibilities that define any time in culture are going to permeate experience and understanding of every sort. It suggests that every kind of understanding is a product of how we understand; and how, specifically, we are capable of understanding at any particular point in time. Thus, we should expect to see related dynamics even with the more "arm's length" considerations of science.

One particular example raises interesting questions in this regard, and only history can tell how its conclusions will hold up. This is the current notion in physics that there may be an infinity of universes, one for every popular reality. Some physicists claim that mathematics supports this conclusion. While the math is beyond my grasp, I can't help but be struck by the parallels with postmodern anything-goes conclusions in which everyone gets their own reality. Here the conclusion is not just psychological, but assumes how reality works on the grandest of scales.

Radical Perspective for Understanding History, Warts and All—From Progress and Wonder to War and Oppression

I've emphasized how learning to think contextually will have ever greater pertinence in times ahead. In a culturally mature reality, we better see how truth at one time or place may be very different from what is true at another. We can think of Creative Systems Theory as a detailed framework for understanding context.

We are not used to thinking contextually. The political Right and the political Left each fails at this essential task today, certainly when it comes to temporal context: Each in its own way neglects to appreciate that realities change and evolve.

This is most obvious with the Right. "Originalism" as a basis for interpreting the U.S. Constitution explicitly denies that change could have any significance. While its sentiments contribute to systemic thinking by resisting radical changes that might occur at the whims of a particular time; in application, right-wing thinking reflects a startling blindness to how living systems work. The fact of systemic change is no small matter. At the time of the framing of the Constitution, people went without indoor plumbing, much less computers and cell phones; and technological advances are the least of it. The changes that the courts need most to take into account have to do with human values—essential changes reshaping how we think about what matters, and what it means to act in accord with what matters. When we assume that such changes will not be seen as significant, it guarantees that our thinking will be naive at best; damaging at worst.

In contrast, those on the Left tend to assume that their "progressive" politics are specifically allied with change. But in today's highly polarized world, liberals in fact do no better. Most immediately, they tend to judge the past in terms of the values of the present. Left populist ideology often dismisses— even condemns—the past. It points out (accurately) that, while the Bill of Rights claimed equality, it did not give women the right to vote; and that George Washington, along with the majority of the founding fathers, were slave holders. These are important observations if we are to fully understand history. But taken out of temporal context, they result in a self-righteous, cynicism-producing picture in which any celebration of historical accomplishments—and certainly any claim of exceptional achievement—is seen only as delusion and evidence of continuing oppression.

The Left also exhibits a sweeping failure to appreciate the dimension of time. They can ascribe to their own version of "originalism" that is arguably even more egregious than that of the Right, in that it goes farther back in time and tends to be covert. Often they romanticize the worldviews of earlier periods in culture—such as the beliefs of indigenous peoples, or those of historical times when more archetypally feminine values prevailed (as with early agrarian societies). Important truths are implied in such sentiments—Creative Systems Theory affirms the fact that important understandings have been lost with progress. But by in effect turning the traditional telling of history on its head, such views further create a naive, self-serving, cynical picture that negates human accomplishment. In the end, they only get in the way of where we need to go. By implication, they make progress itself a problem.

Creative Systems Theory argues that we can think usefully only if we can effectively place our ideas in the context of time. It also clarifies how it is in the nature of cultural systems that they grow and evolve and do so in understandable ways. One characteristic of the new cultural chapter needed—and becoming newly possible—in our time is that it makes it possible to better appreciate the role of change. This includes not only how change works—including its sometimes painful and often unfair consequences; but also the particular kinds of change that will be increasingly important for a healthy future.

I've been thinking a lot lately about the way Creative Systems Theory helps us rethink history. The theory's contribution proves powerful for getting beyond current battles between traditional historical views that emphasize progress and more revisionist interpretations that focus on harm and hypocrisies. It also has major implications for those who would like to move past the polarizing traps of identity politics. And it invites us to rethink the blame-based assumptions of victim narratives wherever we find them.

To get there, we first need to step back and appreciate what the theory adds to our understanding of history. I've written extensively about how the theory lets us map the evolving contours of culture's story. Today, even the basic idea that culture evolves can be controversial; but from the perspective of Creative Systems Theory, that conclusion becomes hard to deny. For example, regarding religion, the theory describes an easily recognizable progression—from animism, to polytheism, to fundamentalist monotheism, to more liberal monotheism. It also provides explanation for what we are seeing in our time. Creative Systems Theory's ability to provide such perspective is a product of the theory's thesis that history is a creative/formative process that organizes in ways that parallel other human creative/formative processes. (The Appendix fills out this thesis.)

A more specific implication of this approach to understanding history is that it helps us get beyond former polarized ways of understanding the past. It looks squarely at historical atrocities; and by making atrocities more understandable, it is possible to psychologically move beyond them.

The story that Creative Systems Theory's picture of cultural chapters describes is not just one of some elegant progression of realities. Along with new possibilities, each stage involves blind spots—even cruelties. Some of these less-than-pleasant characteristics are specific to particular times. For example, human sacrifice and even cannibalism were common in early cultural times. Slavery has been more the rule than the exception until relatively recently. Other fallibilities that have been present throughout history must be revisited in our time. I think in particular of our persistent need to divide our worlds into "chosen people" and "evil others," the psychological dynamic that has made war an ever-present part of the human narrative.

This recognition has powerful consequences if we take it in deeply. Most immediately, it helps us put atrocities into perspective. For example, because my background is Irish, I could very easily hold deep animosities toward the English. Few people fully appreciate how profoundly the English oppressed the Irish over centuries. But understood systemically, it is also the case that this kind of oppression is what we predictably see with the comparative cultural stages the Irish and English peoples occupied. This is not in any way to diminish the very real oppression and harm, or to forgive it. But understood in this way, I can understand it as a historical dynamic and a human one. Today, rather than seeing the English simply as evil people, I can appreciate both their historical blindnesses and their historical contributions.

In some instances, larger perspective gives historical circumstances whole new meaning. For example, I've proposed that it is important to avoid thinking simplistically about the wearing of the hijab or burka in certain counties in the Middle East. Interpreted through modern eyes, such garments seem to be instruments of repression; but seen through a developmental lens, they hold a more complex and interesting significance. With today's modern realities, for many women this kind of attire has stopped serving any historical function and has thus become specifically oppressive. But historically it served to protect not just men, but also women and society from the dynamics that could undermine well-being.[12]

Seeing history through this kind of developmental lens is more than most people are ready for: It requires the recognition that life is more complex and nuanced than we might want to assume. It also requires an acceptance that existence, by its nature, is not just hard, but sometimes fundamentally unfair and often simply brutal. But in my experience, being able to step back in this way is immensely empowering, and in a way that holds particular significance in our time. I've described how grievance-based, victim narratives shape

---

[12] It is a topic that I explore in depth in my book On the Evolution of Intimacy (ICD Press, 2019).

assumptions today, on both the Right and the Left. Groups of every sort see themselves as oppressed and identify some other group as their oppressors, often with historical justification. But this way of thinking ultimately obstructs the path forward. Habitually blaming another for one's misfortunes gets in the way of the mature authority needed for effective leadership today.

The systemic perspective that Creative Systems Theory provides requires that we think in ways that we formerly were not ready for. But, in the end, what it does, is simply help us better see things for what they are and always have been. This is very different from concluding that "everything happens for a reason" or "things are happening just as they should." It in no way dismisses or forgives historical injustices; in fact, the theory judges them harshly, but in a way that takes the dimension of time into account. (For example, while it can make human sacrifice comprehensible in its original temporal context, the same act in our time becomes barbaric and likely evidence of insanity.)[13] And it specifically emphasizes that further steps will be necessary for times ahead on the planet to be tolerable, much less fulfilling. The essential recognition is that the more we can hold the larger story of how things work, the better we can be at making the kinds of creative choices on which our future depends.

---

[13]   Notice that including the dimension of time invites reflection when it comes to slavery. For me, it doesn't change conclusions. But it does open the door to a more nuanced conversation. The recognition that slavery was commonplace in early cultures (including African cultures) helps us get beyond thinking only in terms of good and evil. But slavery when introduced into the New World must be considered well beyond its time of legitimacy—particularly in the context of the Declaration of Independence's claim that "all men are created equal."

CHAPTER SIX

Absurdity's Antidote

Certain insights and methodologies prove particularly helpful if we wish to get beyond Transitional Absurdities and begin to engage Cultural Maturity's systemic world of experience. Here we look at a small handful of them. We can think of the concept of Transitional Absurdity itself as a tool for moving forward. When combined with an understanding of culturally mature perspective and its importance, it alerts us to when we have become trapped in dead-end conclusions. There are also all the needed new capacities that I have touched on with previous reflections, each of which can be practiced. In addition, we can draw on recognitions that, by their nature, challenge us to engage the whole of our cognitive complexity and intelligence's creative multiplicity. I'll briefly touch on the power that comes from appreciating temperament diversity. Finally, I will briefly introduce the "hands-on" methodology that I find works most reliably to produce culturally mature understanding.

Knowledge as Antidote

The inquiries addressed in this book are particularly important kind of antidote. Being able to recognize certain reactive behaviors as Transitional Absurdities and appreciate them as such takes us a long ways toward getting beyond them. And understanding how Cultural Maturity might be an option—perhaps the only viable option—both helps us understand how Transitional Absurdities leave us short and why overcoming them might be important. Other more particular Creative Systems Theory concepts we've applied here, such as the notion of Capacitance and an appreciation for the workings of polar fallacies, help bring detail to our thinking. And those who wish even more conceptual nuance will find Creative Systems notions that address contextual patterns helpful—from the theory's mapping of understanding's evolution through historical times, to ways that it makes more here-and-now systemic relationship more understandable.

Capacities

Over the course of this book, I've referred to a number of capacities needed to effectively address challenges before us. I've suggested that, in each case, they become newly possible, and fully understandable only with Cultural Maturity's cognitive changes. I've addressed a few in some detail, such as the importance of taking responsibility not just for our actions but also for the truths we apply; the ability to "bridge" polar assumptions and think more systemically; and learning to recognize and tolerate limits. And I've touched on others, like the importance of better acknowledging uncertainty and complexity, and the power of learning to think in ways that take context into account. Importantly, in each case, these are capacities we can practice. We can notice how any capacity comes into play with most every kind of challenge when we engage the challenge systemically. And we can take particular issues and appreciate how in every case each of these capacities is pertinent. By building our conceptual muscles in this way we can benefit greatly.

There is one new capacity that I have not labeled as such, but which has been central in these reflections. Creative Systems Theory speaks of the importance of recognizing and directly addressing Questions of Referent. We appropriately ask what truth becomes when we leave behind the culturally prescribed, parental truths of times past. I've described how Integrative Meta-perspective makes it possible to understand with the whole of who we are. In so doing, it invites us to answer weighty questions with a directness that has not before been an option.

At a personal level, the new and deeper ability to address questions of value provides an antidote to today's Crisis of Purpose. When I work with a young person whose life has become aimless, I inquire—first from one direction and then from another—what in his or her unique life creates happiness or meaning. As the person may have forgotten that anything does, I persist. Over the weeks, I make it the question in the room that ultimately matters. As the person finally begins to offer answers, just as doggedly I present a challenge. I have the person make that thing they have begun to articulate as the Referent— the "North Star" for their lives. I challenge them to see what in their lives serves to further the things that most matter to them. I also challenge them to cut out of their lives anything that undermines or coopts that which most matters.

This description should sound familiar. Earlier I discussed how this kind of questioning provides the most reliable treatment approach for addiction: A person needs to get to a place where they are unwilling to accept artificial substitutes for real fulfillment. But I've also noted how aimlessness and addiction have today all too often become the norm. Asking Questions of Referent in our lives necessarily lies at the heart of everyday mental health. And if we are beginning to bring culturally mature capacities into our lives, we become able to answer those questions with a depth and nuance that has not before been an option. The importance of redefining wealth and progress has parallels. This new capacity—and imperative—applies not just personally, but to collective decisions of all sorts. It is what we must repeatedly come back to if we are to continue to survive and thrive as a species.

Reengagement

Another tool for getting beyond Transitional Absurdity is not quite a capacity, but is needed for almost any capacity to be realized. I've noted how the Dilemma of Trajectory leaves us distanced, sometimes estranged from important aspects of who we are. That includes connectedness in our bodies, the more childlike aspects of ourselves, our relationship to nature, spiritual sensibilities, and our capacity to be deeply receptive.

Taking the time to reengage any of these aspects of ourselves can provide an important antidote to Cultural Absurdity. This must be done with some care, particularly if we are at all vulnerable to Unity Fallacies. People can confuse regression with the larger acceptance of life that Cultural Maturity is about, which is but a further version of Transitional Absurdity. But spending time in nature, becoming more intimate with one's body, and simply being more receptively attentive to the everyday world tend to be in themselves good things. And if one is beginning to engage Integrative Meta-perspective, it may provide some of missing pieces that whole-box-of-crayons understanding requires.

Exercising Intelligence's Creative Multiplicity

I ended Chapter Four by describing how human intelligence has multiple aspects and how a key result of Integrative Meta-perspective is the ability to draw on the whole of that multiplicity in more conscious and encompassing ways. My book *Intelligence's Creative Multiplicity: And Its Critical Role in the Future of Understanding* is about grasping the essential implications of doing so. The book not only helps us better understand intelligence's aspects; it provides exercises that can help deepen a person's relationship with them. As with specific new capacities, we can practice a deeper engagement with intelligence's multiple aspects.

Drawing on Temperament Diversity

Creative Systems Theory includes a framework for understanding personality/temperament diversity. The Creative Systems Personality Typology provides a way to understand not just the specific strengths and weaknesses of personality styles, but also how different styles can best work together. It also offers an encompassing framework for understanding how personality diversity interplays with other kinds of human difference, such as age, gender, and ethnic/racial diversity. It has particular significance as a tool for supporting the kind of creative collaboration on which a healthy future will depend. This is another topic about which I've written its own book, *The Creative Systems Theory Personality Typology: Engaging the Generative Roots of Diversity*.

Of particular pertinence to this book's reflections is that deeper understanding of personality differences helps us deal more effectively with conflict. Polarized views commonly reflect not just differences of belief, but differences over which personality style "reality" prevails. Expanding on this observation brings us to what is perhaps the most significant reason for understanding temperament diversity. I've noted how the essential challenges of our time are frequently Whole-System concerns. Because of this, addressing the challenges effectively will require the collaborative input of all the various perspectives that make up human experience—scientists and artists, liberals and conservatives, thinkers and feelers, and so on. Successfully engaging as a species in the tasks before us will require a major leap in our understanding of, and sensitivity to, the very different ways that people organize experience.

Reflections from my years leading yearlong trainings at the Institute for Creative Development provide concrete illustration of this more encompassing contribution. I would select participants for programs according to a couple of criteria: People would need to have enough capacity to be "up to the task." But just as important was personality style: I chose participants with the goal of fully representing temperament diversity. On the first day of training, people immediately noticed how different were the individuals in the room from the people they usually spent time with. Because these were individuals of universally high capacity, such differences could not easily be dismissed.

Having that diversity—and that particular kind of diversity—in the room was powerful at a personal level. A person may never be a jazz musician, a professional football player, or an advertising executive; but if the person can begin to understand what makes such people who they are—and better, to slightly embody their felt realities—the presence of those others can help a person engage creation's full systemic complexity. Partway through the year, I would engage the group in a deep immersion into the Creative Systems Personality Typology to help make these learnings more conscious.

Having that particular kind of diversity in the room also became essential for the group's shared work. The mosaic of realities represented by personality style differences supported the collaborative efforts needed to address the deeply systemic questions these emerging culturally mature leaders were there to engage. Near the end of the training, I would have participants divide into small think-tank teams to work on the future of specific domains—education, government, business, education, science, religion, and so on. By that time, they had come to recognize that choosing like-minded team members was not the right approach if they wanted culturally mature results. If participants' teams were going to be most powerfully creative, they would need the contributions of each basic temperament axis.

Parts Work

The most direct means I know to get beyond Transitional Absurdity and support culturally mature understanding is an approach I call simply Parts Work. Parts Work treats our various aspects—the crayons in our internal creative box—like characters in a play. It engages people in learning to appreciate and effectively draw on all these various aspects/characters. In the process, people learn to hold and creatively manage the whole of who they are and the whole of any question they might wish to address.

Parts Work begins with a person choosing a question or concern to explore. The person, sitting in what will eventually be his or her Whole-Person chair (Personally Mature Perspective chair—or perhaps, eventually, Culturally

Mature Perspective chair), is then guided in placing various parts around the room—perhaps a curious part, an angry part, a reasonable part, an intellectual part, a sexual part. Each part is given its own chair (Figure 6-1). Through engaging in conversation with the various parts, the person learns to consciously draw on and apply his or her larger—whole-box-of-crayons—complexity.

Fig. 6-1. Parts Work

Three related cardinal rules guide the Parts Work process, each tying directly to how our cognitive mechanisms become different with Integrative Meta-perspective. The first rule: The Whole-Person chair (or Whole-System Perspective chair with larger cultural issues) provides the leadership in a culturally mature reality (Figure 6-2). It is the Whole-Person chair that interacts with the world. And the Whole-Person chair, through interacting with each of the parts, draws on their contributions. This rule makes doing Parts Work a hands-on exercise for practicing culturally mature leadership—in oneself and in the world.

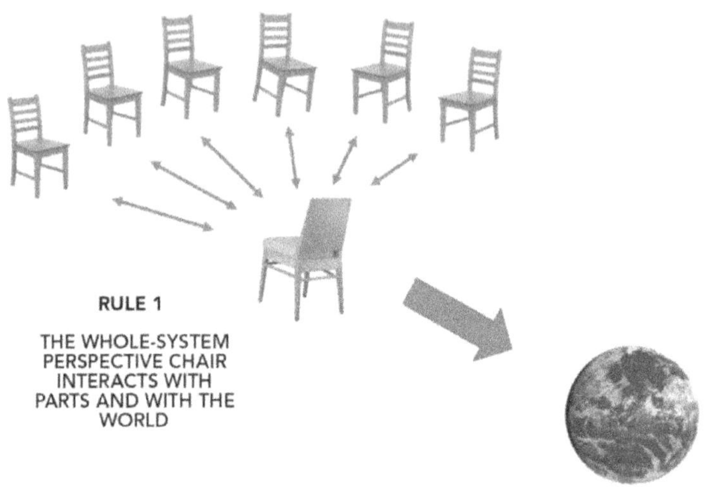

Fig. 6-2. Only the Whole-Person Chair Interacts with Parts and with the World

The second rule follows from the first: Parts do not interact with the world (Figure 6-3). A person doing Parts Work quickly recognizes that engaging the world from parts—what most people do most of the time—produces limited and limiting results. People also come to recognize that their ideological beliefs, whether political, religious, or competing belief systems within their professions, involve parts taking over and acting as if they have a relationship with the world.

Fig. 6-3. Parts Don't Talk to the World

The third cardinal rule: Parts don't talk to other parts (Figure 6-4). This recognition can take a bit longer to grasp, but it is just as critical. Much in the internal struggles of daily life is crosstalk between competing parts, and the implications are just as significant collectively. Parts talking to parts cause us to confuse moderation or compromise with culturally mature perspective. In addition, certain kinds of ideological beliefs have their roots in parts talking to parts. Creative Systems Theory describes how we can understand the back-and-forth between competing worldviews over the course of history as conversations between systemic parts.

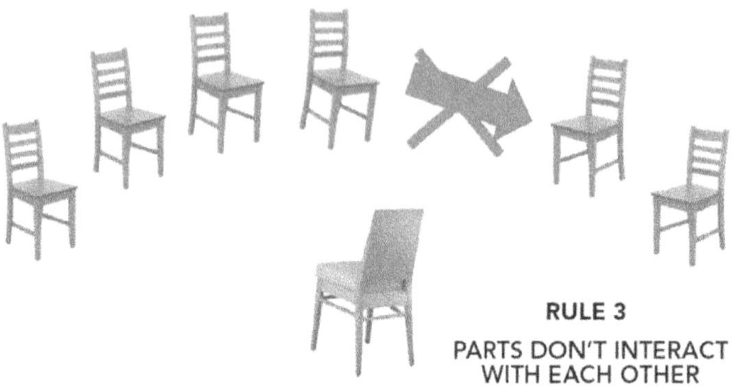

Fig. 6-4. Parts Don't Talk to Other Parts

The result when one follows these cardinal rules is a kind of "cognitive rewiring" (Figure 6-5): Wires between parts, and between parts and the world, are severed. At the same time, people strengthen the wires that connect themselves with the world, and themselves with their diversely creative contributing parts. Key to the power of the Parts Work approach is that the person does not need to be conscious of why it is working. Get the wiring right and culturally mature understanding and culturally mature leadership capacities naturally result.

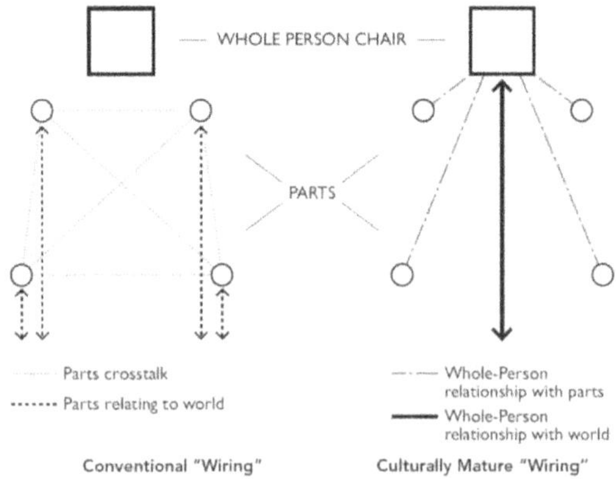

Fig. 6-5. Cultural Maturity's Cognitive "Rewiring"

One result of Parts Work is the possibility of obtaining answers to the questions raised at the work's starting point. But more important is the practice gained in holding experience more systemically. Through the dual process of simultaneously exercising authority from the Whole-Person chair and drawing deeply on the diverse viewpoints that the parts represent, the person becomes increasingly facile at engaging experience in more conscious and complete ways. When this work is done at a personal level, the person learns both to take more conscious authority in life and to draw more deeply on the diverse sensibilities that make them the unique person they are. When the work happens at a more cultural level, Parts Work engages the person in drawing consciously and deeply on the diverse sensibilities and inclinations that make us who we are as humans.

Parts Work is not a "quick fix," even if the focus is primarily on concerns of a more personal sort. But engaged over time, more encompassing ways of thinking and acting follow naturally from the process. Ultimately Parts Work alters not just how a person engages specific issues, but also how he or she engages reality more broadly. The work becomes like lifting weights to build the "muscles" of culturally mature capacity.

Parts Work can also be used to engage overarching questions more systemically. For example, in my book *Creative Systems Theory*, I describe how it can help reconcile the most fundamental and timeless of polarities—that which divides the material and the spiritual: science and religion. When done well, the way that Parts Work equally challenges the assumptions of those who identify with either scientific or religious conclusions further highlights how culturally mature perspective is new in a fundamental sense. It also provides a good illustration of the power of Parts Work.

Someone of a more scientific bent doing Parts Work is likely, at least initially, to assume that the part that thinks rationally and scientifically should sit in the Whole-Person/Whole-System chair. This is not an unreasonable assumption given where the person has often most found significance. But before too long it becomes clear that there are many concerns of no small importance, particularly in one's personal life, such as purpose or love, where that one part is limited in what is has to contribute. Eventually the person comes to recognize that more than this one part is needed—not just for making good life choices, but for the most filled-out and creative kind of science.

Something very similar tends to happen for people who identify with spiritual inclinations. This may be an individual either with traditional religious beliefs, with more humanistic "spiritual but not religious" tendencies, or someone with a New Age bent. Commonly the person will assume that spiritual truth appropriately sits in the Whole-Person/Whole-System chair. And again, for them, this is not an unreasonable conclusion. But if the person of more spiritual/religious inclination works long enough, they recognize that, in our time, spiritual truth sitting in the Whole-Person/Whole-System chair leads to problems similar to those encountered by the science-minded individual. An all-too-common result is poorly-thought-out life choices and unsuccessful relationships. It turns out that in a well-lived life—a spiritual life in the best sense—the more manifest parts of existence are as important as the essences. Eventually, the person may realize that holding the spiritual more systemically in this way will be key not just to making good everyday choices, but to the most full and creative relationship with spiritual experience.

In doing Parts Work, the chairs that advocate for aspects of larger truths—whether personal truths or truths of a more social or even philosophical sort—each in important ways adds to the Whole-Person/Whole-System Perspective chair's reflections. But they function at best as consultants. When we miss this fact, unhelpful, indeed dangerous ideological conclusions result. In Parts Work, people confront this recognition not just as some abstract conclusion, but immediately at a personal level. Living from the Whole-Person/Whole-System chair is the ultimate task of culturally mature leadership, whether in our personal lives or more broadly. This perspective ultimately defines today's needed new common sense.

AFTERWORD

Returning to the Question

The concept of Transitional Absurdity is necessarily more a question than an answer; but it may be the question on which our future human well-being most depends. If the concept is not correct, then some of the concerns I have touched on in these pages could easily be the end of us. We could be facing a future that is brutish and devoid of meaning.

If the concept of Transitional Absurdity is accurate, there is at least a way forward. We can also better understand what going forward effectively will require of us. In addition, we can better appreciate how going forward could be not just positive, but with the idea of a needed growing up as a species, an important kind of realization.

The Evidence

A radical concept like Transitional Absurdity requires good evidence. Given that ironclad evidence is lacking, however, we must look to more indirect means of confirmation.

Evidence becomes important both when addressing immediate concerns and with regard to big-picture considerations. The first kind of needed evidence relates to whether the concept of Transitional Absurdity might apply in any one particular situation. I've described how the concept can easily become a repository for any phenomenon that a person's particular worldview might find aversive. People can also use the concept to dismiss phenomena that are not appropriately seen in this way with comments like, "Oh, that is just a

Transitional Absurdity," and in the process missing where solutions lie. Sometimes we can recognize right off that the concept of Transitional Absurdity is not pertinent. But we might also see that it provides important guidance.

Bigger-picture evidence of Transitional Absurdity addresses whether the concept is ultimately correct. In the end, the evidence can only be the kind I have offered here—that of conceptual prediction, observed pattern, and the evidence of seeking the explanation that is most consistent with what we see. The big-picture perspective offered by Creative Systems Theory and the common themes across realms of understanding that this book has examined offer suggestions.

Perhaps the most important evidence is indirect: the relationship to hope. Today's realities are often unpleasant if not crazy, and they do not seem to bode well. For many people they seem only to point toward a dystopian future. I've noted how the concept of Transitional Absurdity is not the only interpretation that is consistent with hope. If all we are seeing is the kind of two-steps-forward-one-step-back dynamic common with social change, we might with time simply get back on track.

But in combination with the concept of Cultural Maturity, the result is not merely hopeful; it is this in a particularly consequential way. I've described how the concept of Transitional Absurdity is not only consistent with hope, but that it also points toward new possibilities. And the possibility of Cultural Maturity can be realized only if we bring sufficient awareness and courage to the task. Creative Systems Theory describes how the potential for Cultural Maturity's changes is developmentally built into who we are. And there is the final recognition that the place where Cultural Maturity's changes take us is not only needed for our well-being; it also reflects an essential kind of human realization.

Being that you are part of the larger system undergoing these changes, you could think of your own response in reading previous chapters as a kind of evidence. If you have found that what I have suggested basically makes sense, that it at least supports the importance of the question. And if it inspires you to act in solutions, then it has at least served a creative purpose.

Why the Concept of Transitional Absurdity is Important

The book's look at specific kinds of Transitional Absurdities lets us expand on previous reflections on how the concept can help us. How the concept of Transition Absurdity is worth our time should now be clearer.

At the very least, the concept of Transitional Absurdity alerts us to the severity of current dangers and provides insights into how current thinking often fails us. Like water is to fish, we can miss much that is most important to recognize in our time. Without looking squarely at our absurdities, it is very unlikely that we will find a way beyond them.

We've looked at how social concerns such as suicide, homelessness, addiction, and gun violence can be understood, rather than as separate concerns, as symptoms of a larger Crisis of Purpose that by itself could be our undoing. We've seen how today's increasing polarization and regression in the face of new challenges makes not only effective governance, but the possibility of simply getting along, hard to imagine. We've also examined how techno-utopian notions and ultimately any belief that extends the Modern Age story puts us at risk. And we've looked at how postmodern notions, which might seem to take us forward, at best take us only part way and at worst increase the dangers and craziness. Put simply, the concept of Transitional Absurdity alerts us to the fact that a major portion of what people do and say in our time is not merely absurd—it is dangerously so.

The concept of Transitional Absurdity also helps us make sense of some of the disturbing phenomena that I have described. It is more than a question of simple academic interest. Recognizing that Transitional Absurdities are understandable and predictable can prevent their being the end of us.

At the least, it makes them less overwhelming and helps us respond more constructively to crazy circumstances, as poor responses to Transitional Absurdities easily amplify the absurdities and the dangers. It is quite possible that the human experience will come to an end not because of malevolence, but because we become overwhelmed and respond irrationally to otherwise manageable situations.

Recognizing that Transitional Absurdities are understandable can also help us in a more everyday way. Transitional Absurdities can distract us, leaving us vulnerable to getting sidetracked from our precious creative energies. We can get caught up in the lunacy of political soap operas, or become irate over some contentious issue. Such responses are understandable; and certainly, it is important to speak out when we encounter craziness. But responding reactively is seldom a good use of attention and resources. When we miss the larger picture, our reactions can feed into—and prolong—the absurdity. Our task is to keep our eyes on what most matters and to support propitious solutions when we find them. This maturity of response asks more of a person, but in the end, it is what produces actions that make a difference.

Which brings us to the greatest benefit we can gain from the concept of Transitional Absurdity: It alerts us to what will be needed going forward. I've identified the ultimate antidote to each kind of unpleasantness we have explored. It is, in the end, Cultural Maturity and the sophisticated ways of thinking and acting that it makes possible.

This recognition points toward needed concrete actions. I've observed that Cultural Maturity demands—and makes possible—new kinds of capacities. Transitional Absurdities emphasize the need for these new capacities— whether it is a more mature relationship to limits, the ability to get beyond the either/or thinking of times past, or the application of more accurate measures of progress. Importantly, these are new capacities that we can practice.

Looking at the big picture, Transitional Absurdities make us confront what is needed in our time, giving clarity to Cultural Maturity. Scrutinizing the various forms of Transitional Absurdities makes obvious that Culture Maturity's notion of "growing up" as a species is very different than some utopian future. Rather, it is about an important, natural next step in what it means to be human. I've spoken of Cultural Maturity as a needed "new common sense," which is an even more human kind of result; but it is arguably, also a more profound one.

We can think of the concept of Transitional Absurdity as an essential tool in the culturally mature leader's tool bag. Understood with depth and subtlety, it helps make sense of much that might otherwise only confuse or disturb; and in ways that help us get beyond ideological, easy answers and recognize where needed solutions lie.

Looking Forward

The fact that Transitional Absurdities, when carried into the future, become insane raises the question of what we should anticipate in the decades ahead. While Cultural Maturity suggests important new possibilities, Transitional dynamics suggest something quite different if the absurdities continue to any great degree; and, in fact, they most likely will. At any major culture change point, we tend to hold onto old realities well beyond their timeliness. This is pretty much how things work—partly out of fear and denial, partly because systems are not homogeneous. There will always be great diversity in the rates of transition among individual people.

My hope is that this book's reflections have offered perspective for navigating through what may often be disturbing and difficult times. Particularly important is the recognition that the concept of Transitional Absurdity is as much about possibility as it is about craziness. And it is possible, not only that we might survive and perhaps thrive; but that we could live in a future that is significant, if not profound.

We may well need to confront much that is quite insane in times ahead. But we can take comfort in the guidance implied by the concept of Transitional Absurdity. No matter how bumpy the road ahead, the task remains straightforward: We need to engage the perspective—indeed, the wisdom—that Cultural Maturity's more encompassing vantage provides.

APPENDIX

Creative Systems Theory and the Concept of Cultural Maturity

Many readers will appreciate an introduction to Creative Systems Theory and the concept of Cultural Maturity. In the piece that follows, I provide additional background and touch briefly on many of its main observations while describing the basis for the typology. Think of these reflections as adding flesh to previous bare-boned conceptual observations. You can find a more extended introduction in my book, *Insight: Creative Systems Theory's Radical New Picture of Human Possibility*.[14]

Background

Creative Systems Theory began in attempts to better understand the workings of creative processes. In time it evolved into an overarching framework for understanding purpose, change, and interrelationship in human systems. The theory has its foundation in the recognition that our meaning-making, toolmaking—we could say simply "creative"—nature is what ultimately defines us.

Creative Systems Theory concepts help us step back and appreciate culture's larger story, how human understanding has evolved over time. That includes not only the evolution of belief, but also the changing cognitive structures that have produced those beliefs. And specifically, it includes

---

14   Charles M. Johnston, MD, Insight: Creative Systems Theory's Radical New Picture of Creative Possibility, ICD Press, 2022.

changes that reorder understanding in our time. The theory's comprehensive framework offers a way to replace Modern Age mechanistic thinking with ideas that better reflect that we are alive, and alive in the particular way that makes us human.

The concept of Cultural Maturity follows from Creative Systems Theory's larger picture. Much of my life's work has involved attempting to make sense of critical challenges ahead for our species, focusing less on technical challenges than on human challenges. Central to these efforts has been the observation that effectively addressing many of the most important of these challenges will require new kinds of human abilities. When I recognized that the potential for these new abilities was built into who we are, that observation shifted from an obstacle to something more consistent with hope: We don't have to invent them from whole cloth. The Creative Systems concept of Cultural Maturity describes the core task of our time as a new—and newly possible—"growing up" as a species.[15] Cultural Maturity involves changes not only in what we think, but in how we think, making essential new abilities possible. They also make possible new ways of thinking, as in terms of Creative Systems Theory.

My efforts over the years have approached the ideas of Creative Systems Theory and the concept of Cultural Maturity from multiple directions. I've endeavored to clarify their essential roles in helping us address future questions in all parts of our lives—from the challenges of effective leadership and governance to what love and human relationships will require of us. With my direction of the Institute for Creative Development (a Seattle-based think tank and center for advanced leadership training), I worked for twenty-five years to teach and foster culturally mature leadership. I've written over a dozen books

---

[15]   I first introduced Creative Systems Theory and the concept of Cultural Maturity with my 1984 book The Creative Imperative: Human Growth and Planetary Evolution (Celestial Arts). The book Creative Systems Theory: A Comprehensive Theory of Purpose, Change, and Interrelationship in Human Systems (ICD Press, 2021) provides the most detailed description of the theory.

and numerous articles that expand on the ideas of Creative Systems Theory and the broader implications of culturally mature understanding.

Here I will touch briefly on the shift in perspective that Creative Systems Theory represents. I will then turn more specifically to the concept of Cultural Maturity and examine some of the new human capacities Cultural Maturity's changes make possible. I will take a closer look at some of Creative Systems Theory's more detailed formulations. Finally, I will give particular attention to the implications of these notions for future leadership and summarize the evidence that supports what I have described.

The Power of a Creative Frame

The insight that makes Creative Systems Theory's more detailed formulations wholly new is the power of a creative frame. We can consider a creative frame as following directly from Cultural Maturity's cognitive reordering. Thinking in creative terms provides a Fundamental Organizing Concept, able to take us beyond machine model notions from times past. In a related way, the application of a creative frame also transcends romantic and idealist objections to mechanistic notions.

Creative Systems Theory includes three basic kinds of "patterning concepts" —notions that help us think about truth in ways that better reflect that we are living beings—with each kind of patterning concept having its foundation in a creative reframing of cognition. Patterning in Time concepts concern truth's temporal relativity. They address change processes in human systems—the dynamics of innovation, individual development, the growth of relationships, and, of particular importance, the evolution of culture. Patterning in Space notions address here-and-now contextual relativity. We can use them to help make sense of inner psychological dynamics as well as the workings of larger systems, from families and organizations to nations. Of the Patterning in Space tools, the most fully developed is the Creative Systems Personality

Typology. The third group of notions, what the theory calls Whole-Person/Whole-System patterning concepts, addresses more general questions of possibility, motivation, and capacity.

Cultural Maturity

The Creative Systems Theory concept of Cultural Maturity focuses specifically on today. It presents a new guiding narrative, able to replace Modern Age assumptions that increasingly fail to serve us. It also describes new kinds of skills and capacities that will be needed if we are to effectively make our way. And it delineates how the task involves thinking not only new things; but thinking in new, more complete and systemic ways. We can think of culturally mature perspective as providing the future's needed "new common sense." Creative Systems Theory's overarching formulations reflect this more mature and complete kind of perspective.

The concept of Cultural Maturity is not as easy a notion as the simple phrase "growing up" might suggest. For most people, it challenges favorite assumptions and requires us to think in more encompassing ways than we are used to. But where it takes us is ultimately straightforward. In thinking of the changes that produce culturally mature understanding, I find it helpful to divide the process into a couple of steps. In the end, these steps reflect aspects of a single mechanism; but looking at them separately assists us in getting started.

The first change process gives the concept its name. Cultural Maturity brings a new, more mature relationship between culture and the individual. In times past, culture has functioned as a parent in the lives of individuals, providing us with clear rules to live by. Cultural absolutes offered not only a sense of shared identity and connectedness with others; they also protected us from life's persistent uncertainties and immense complexities.

Today, this traditional relationship is changing. As cultural absolutes lose their ability to serve us as they once did, their influence is diminishing.

However, this loss of past collective rules has Janus-faced implications: While it can reveal possibilities that before now we could not have considered, at the same time it can create a disturbing void. Clearly something more is needed. If all that is happening today is the loss of past parental guideposts, we have problems. With nothing to replace them, we are left with the postmodern, anything-goes, everybody-gets-their-own-truth notion. What might look like freedom would instead result only in disorder and dangerous aimlessness.

The second kind of change process is what makes today's loss of past absolutes something to celebrate. It turns out that the same change mechanisms that generate the rejection of traditional cultural truths also create the potential for new, more mature ways of understanding. But Cultural Maturity is more than just "acting grown-up." It involves developmentally predicted cognitive changes. We might think of culturally mature thought as "post-postmodern."

Creative Systems Theory uses an ungainly (but quite precise) term for the cognitive reordering that gives us Cultural Maturity and its new vantage for understanding: Integrative Meta-perspective. Integrative Meta-perspective involves, first, a more complete kind of stepping back from our complex natures, which creates greater awareness. It is also what creates new distance from culture's past parental role. At the same time, Cultural Maturity's cognitive changes involve a new and deeper engagement with the whole of our cognitive complexity, all the diverse aspects of who we are. The result is not merely further abstraction; it is the fully-embodied kind of understanding that is needed for mature decision-making.[16]

We will return presently to this point for a closer look. For now, it is enough to appreciate that Integrative Meta-perspective allows us to think in ways that are more encompassing and complete than was previously possible.

---

[16] My book Rethinking How We Think: Integrative Meta-Perspective and the Cognitive "Growing Up" On Which Our Future Depends (ICD Press, 2020) provides a detailed examination of this cognitive reordering.

We could say that this new way of thinking is more systemic—or simply wiser. I often use the metaphor of a box of crayons, the crayons representing systemic aspects while the box represents an encompassing perspective. Integrative Meta-perspective lets us step back and draw more consciously—and deeply— from the whole box.

New Questions and New Human Capacities

I've proposed that addressing the critical questions before us will require new kinds of human capacities. One of the best arguments in support of Cultural Maturity is that its cognitive changes make these needed new capacities possible. Noting a few of these capacities will help affirm the importance of Culturally Maturity's changes and highlight important aspects of where they take us.

Accepting a new kind of responsibility: As we leave behind culture as a symbolic parent, we necessarily assume a new depth of responsibility, both for our actions and the truths we draw on.

Getting beyond the polarizing "us-and-them" attitudes of the past: The obvious importance of this capacity is most apparent in the fact that it helps us leave behind the "chosen people/evil other" polarizations that throughout history have led to war. Creative Systems Theory describes how relationships of all sorts— between nations, defining leadership, pertaining to friendship or love— typically have been based on projection, where we relate not as whole beings, but as dependent halves that together made a whole. Integrative Meta-perspective's more systemic vantage helps us re-own the projections that before had produced mythologized perceptions of both the demonized and idealized sort. With Cultural Maturity's cognitive reordering, we become better able to act in the world as whole systems, and to recognize other systems as whole systems.

Better appreciating the fact of limits: The Modern Age story has been a heroic one; we celebrated a world without limits. Increasingly, however, we recognize that if we are not more attentive to limits, we are doomed. Integrative Meta-perspective's more encompassing vantage makes clear that, whatever our concern, in the end, limits come with the territory. The greater maturity that comes with Integrative Meta-perspective applies to real limits of every sort—limits to what we can do (as with environmental limits); limits to what we can know and predict (as with effective risk assessment), and limits to what we can be for one another (as with culturally mature relationships). It also reveals how a mature acknowledgement of limits, rather than limiting us, in the end increases possibility.

Learning to better tolerate complexity and uncertainty: Today, questions of every kind confront us with new complexities and uncertainties. Because Integrative Meta-perspective draws directly on our own systemic complexity, it helps us tolerate and make sense of complexity in the world around us. And, for a related reason, Cultural Maturity's changes make us more comfortable in uncertainty's presence. Creative Systems Theory describes how ideas become ideological—and thus expressions of last-word truth—when we make one aspect of a larger complexity (one crayon in that systemic box) the whole of understanding. However, when we engage in understanding more fully, uncertainty becomes intrinsic to any deep understanding of truth. Creative Systems Theory goes even further to describe how both complexity and uncertainty are necessary ingredients in cognition's "creative" workings.

Learning to think about what matters in more systemically complete ways: By applying Integrative Meta-perspective we become able to "measure" significance in ways that better reflect the whole of who we are and the whole of anything we might wish to consider. For example, moral decisions become less about choosing between good and evil, and more about acknowledging competing goods and discerning where the most life-affirming choices ultimately lie. And as relationships of all sorts require us to step beyond two-halves-make-a-whole projective dynamics, in a similar way Integrative Meta-perspective lets us more directly discern when a human connection enhances life. This new capacity applies most broadly to the critical task of rethinking advancement. Our times demand that we think about wealth and progress in ways that are more encompassing and complete.

Better understanding how events happen in a context, particularly in the context of our time in culture's story: Thinking that serves us going forward must help us make more dynamic and nuanced kinds of discernments. Of particular importance, it must help us be more attentive to context. With culturally mature truth, the "when" and the "where" are always as important as the "what." Such contextual relativity is wholly different from relativity of the postmodern, anything-goes sort. Culturally mature understanding allows us to make highly precise distinctions that are precise exactly because they take contextual nuances into account. We can think of Creative Systems Theory's framework for understanding purpose, change, and interrelationship in human systems as a set of tools for making such context-specific observations. The Creative Systems Personality Typology is a specific example of this kind of contribution.

Integrative Meta-perspective and Polarity

A closer look at the cognitive reorganization that underlies Cultural Maturity's changes helps us appreciate why such new capacities result, and ties them more directly to Creative Systems Theory's conceptual framework. I've described how Integrative Meta-perspective involves at once more fully stepping back from and more deeply engaging the whole of our human complexity. Reflecting briefly on a couple of ways of thinking about that complexity—the role of polarity in how we think and the fact of intelligence's multiplicity—provides important further insight.

Let's first consider the fact of polarity. Creative Systems Theory describes how each chapter in culture's story to this point has framed truth in terms of qualities set in polar juxtaposition; for example, in modern times, mind versus body, leader versus follower, science versus religion. Robert Frost observed, "It almost scares a man the way things come in pairs." With Cultural Maturity's cognitive reordering, we both step back from and more deeply engage past either/or relationships. In the process, we become able to appreciate them as aspects of larger systemic realities.

Creative Systems Theory brings detail to what we see. As a start, it addresses why we see polarity in the first place. After proposing that the attributes that most make us human are our meaning-making, toolmaking, and "creative" prowess; it goes on to describe how our cognitive mechanisms are designed to support this capacity for innovation. Specifically regarding polarity, it describes how the fact that we think in polar terms follows directly from this creative picture.

Creative Systems Theory delineates how the same progression of polar relationships orders creative/formative change of all sorts—from an act of invention to the evolution of culture. Such change begins with a newly created aspect budding off from its original context. With each succeeding stage in formative process's first half, polar aspects become more separate, juxtaposing in evolving, creatively predicted ways. With the second, more mature half of any formative process, polarities reconcile to create a new and larger whole. We then come to experience the newly created entity as "second nature."

This sequence provides a template for understanding formative process wherever we might find it. Creative Systems Theory calls the generic map that results—applicable to formative dynamics from the most personal of insights to the most encompassing of collective processes—the Creative Function (Figure A-1).

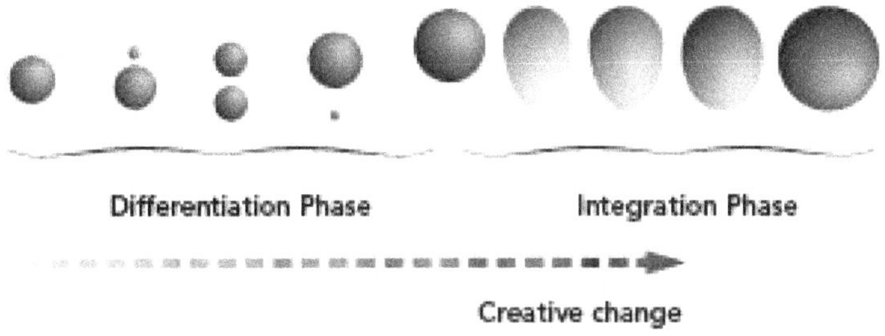

Fig. A-1. The Creative Function

We can recognize this two-part extended picture in personal psychological development. The underlying impetus during development in the first half of an individual life is toward distinction and establishing of identity as form. In childhood we begin discovering who we are, during adolescence we make our first forays into the social world, and over adulthood we establish our unique place in that world. Second-half-of-life maturing involves more integrative tasks: It is about learning how to live in the world with the greatest perspective, depth, and integrity.

On a cultural scale, this picture of evolving polar relationships has critical implications for understanding the times in which we live. I've described Cultural Maturity's "growing up" in our thinking and acting in terms of Integrative Meta-perspective and the more encompassing kind of understanding it makes possible. Integrative Meta-perspective thus helps us get our minds around apparent polar opposites on the largest of scales. The Creative Function helps us appreciate how Cultural Maturity's cognitive reordering is a predicted consequence of our time in culture's evolving creative story.

We don't need Creative Systems Theory's detailed formulations to appreciate the relationship between polarity and Integrative Meta-perspective.

F. Scott Fitzgerald proposed that "the test of a first-rate intelligence is the ability to hold two opposed ideas in the mind at the same time, and still retain the ability to function." (We might substitute "a mature intelligence" for "a first-rate intelligence.") His reference was to personal maturity, but this capacity is such an inescapable part of culturally mature perspective that we could almost say it defines it.

One of the simplest ways to think about the way culturally mature perspective changes how we understand, draws on the basic observation that necessary new understandings of every sort "bridge" polar assumptions of times past.[17] We can think of Cultural Maturity's point of departure as itself a "bridging" dynamic. As we step back and see the relationship of culture and the individual in more encompassing terms, Cultural Maturity "bridges" ourselves and our societal contexts (or, put another way, ourselves and final truth). It is through this fundamental "bridging" that we leave behind society's past parental function.

This encompassing linkage holds within it a multitude of local "bridging." Nothing has characterized the last century's defining conceptual advances more than their linking of previously unquestioned polar truths. Physics 'new picture provocatively circumscribed the realities of matter and energy, space and time, object and observer. New understandings in biology more closely linked humankind with the natural world; and by reopening timeless questions about life's origins, joined the purely physical with the organic. And the ideas of modern psychology, neurology, and sociology have provided an increasingly integrated picture of the workings of conscious with unconscious, mind with body, self with society, and more.

If the relationship between "bridging" and Cultural Maturity is to make

---

17   I organized my early book, Necessary Wisdom: Meeting the Challenge of a New Cultural Maturity (Celestial Arts, 1991), around this basic observation.

useful sense, we need to include a couple of critical distinctions. We need first to clearly distinguish between personal maturity and Cultural Maturity. The ability to hold "opposed ideas," as described by F. Scott Fitzgerald, has been a characteristic of wise thought throughout history. In contrast, none of the last century's defining insights that I just noted would have made sense before now. The "bridging" of cultural realities as described by the concept of Cultural Maturity is a specific phenomenon of our time.

We must also avoid confusing "bridging" as I am using the term with more familiar outcomes (which is why I put the word in quotes). The result is wholly different from averaging or compromise, from walking the white line in the middle of the road. And, just as fundamentally, it is different from simple oneness, the collapsing of one pole into the other that we commonly see with more spiritual interpretations. "Bridging" in this sense is about consciously drawing on the whole creative box of crayons.

Cultural Maturity and Intelligence's Creative Multiplicity

Framing Cultural Maturity's cognitive reordering in terms of intelligence's multiplicity provides further nuance and helps us better put the changes that result—and their significance—in historical perspective. Creative Systems Theory emphasizes the fact that intelligence has multiple parts. Besides our rationality (in which we take appropriate pride), intelligence has other aspects—some more emotional or symbolic; others more sensory.

Most of what Creative Systems Theory has to say about our diverse ways of knowing is beyond the scope of this Appendix;[18] but certain observations are pertinent, particularly Creative Systems Theory's justification for our

---

[18] See Charles M. Johnston, MD, Intelligence's Creative Multiplicity: And Its Critical Role in the Future of Understanding, ICD Press, 2023.

multiple intelligences and its description of how they work together to support and drive our creative proclivities. We find a related intelligence-specific progression with every kind of human formative process—be it invention, individual development, the growth of a relationship, or, of particular importance for these reflections, the evolution of culture. Different aspects of intelligence and different relationships between intelligences are what most define experience at different creative stages.

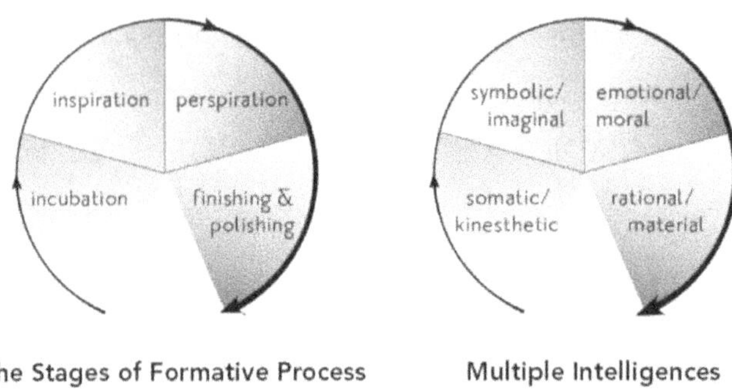

Fig. A-2. Formative Process and Intelligence's Creative Multiplicity

Creative Systems Theory (CST) delineates four basic types of intelligence. For ease of conversation, we can refer to them simply as the intelligences of the body, the imagination, the emotions, and the intellect. (The theory uses the fancier language displayed in Figure A-2.) CST proposes that these different ways of knowing represent more than merely diverse approaches to processing information. They represent the windows through which we make sense of our worlds and the formative tendencies that lead us to shape our worlds in the ways that we do.

This observation has major practical implications. It provides the basis for Creative Systems Theory's framework for understanding the workings of human systems. It also has consequences of a more philosophical and paradigmatic sort. I've hinted at how Creative Systems Theory is significant not only because it provides new conceptual tools for making our way, but also because it successfully takes us beyond the kind of thinking that has defined Modern Age understanding.

Enlightenment thinkers such as Sir Isaac Newton and René Descartes described reality as a great clockwork. While machine-model thinking has made a huge contribution—it has given us not only scientific and industrial advancement, but our modern concept of the individual, as well—it presents real problems if we wish to talk about living systems. There is no more significant conceptual challenge in our time than finding ways to address human systems in living terms. Any culturally mature notion at the least implies this important conceptual leap; but Creative Systems Theory makes it explicit. I've proposed that the creative frame which serves as the theory's foundation represents a new Fundamental Organizing Concept that takes us beyond the mechanistic assumptions of times past. By drawing on this dynamic and generative approach to understanding, the theory can provide highly delineated formulations that directly reflect the fact that we are living—and human—beings.

A more historical look at Integrative Meta-perspective through the lens of intelligence's multiplicity helps fill out the conceptual leap that produces culturally mature understanding. Modern Age thought similarly had its origins in a new cognitive orientation. By stepping back from previous ways of knowing, we grew better able to reject the mystical sensibilities that gave us the beliefs of the Middle Ages.

Along with this general stepping back came a newly central significance to rationality. The rational now stood clearly separate from the subjective aspects of experience and allied with conscious awareness. The result was a new, as-if-from-a-balcony sense of clarity and objectivity. This, combined with the accompanying new belief in the individual as a logical choice-maker, produced all the great advances of the Modern Age.

But while Modern Age thought was a grand achievement, Integrative Meta-perspective's version of stepping back represents a wholly different sort of accomplishment. Awareness comes to stand more fully separate from the whole of our intelligence's systemic complexity—including the rational. Integrative Meta-perspective offers that we might step back equally from aspects of ourselves that we formerly treated as objective as well as those that we had thought of as subjective. In the process, it offers that we might better step back from the whole of intelligence.

And there is more. Culturally mature understanding requires not only that we be aware of intelligence's multiple aspects; but also, in a whole new sense, that we embody each of these aspects. It directly draws on all of our diverse ways of knowing. While culturally mature understanding requires thinking in a rational sense—indeed, it expands rationality's role; just as much it involves more directly plumbing the feeling, imagining, and sensing aspects of who we are. And this is the case for the most rigorous of hard theory as well as our more personal concerns. Making sense of most anything about us—the values we hold, the nature of identity, what it means to have human relationships—increasingly requires this more encompassing kind of understanding.

An important outcome when we frame Cultural Maturity in this way might at first seem contradictory. On one hand, because culturally mature perspective draws on multiple, often conflicting aspects of who we are, its conclusions are less absolute and once-and-for-all than those we are used to. I've described how this perspective requires that we be more comfortable with complexity and uncertainty. But, at the same time, we can appropriately argue that culturally mature understanding is more "objective" than what it replaces. Certainly it is more complete.

During the Enlightenment, thought might have claimed ultimate objectivity, but in fact it was objectivity of only a limited sort. Besides leaving culture's parental status untouched, it left experience divided: objective (in the old sense) as opposed to subjective, mind as opposed to body, thoughts as opposed to feelings, and anything else that does not conform to modernity's rationalist/materialist worldview. We cannot claim to be objective if we have left out half of the evidence. In contrast, culturally mature objectivity is specifically an all-the-crayons-in-the-box sort.

The fact that we can understand Cultural Maturity in terms of developmentally predicted cognitive changes also points toward an important further implication suggested earlier: It supports being legitimately optimistic about what may lie ahead. If Cultural Maturity's cognitive changes are built into who we are as potential, the likelihood that we can thrive and prosper in times ahead increases significantly. And, if this is a cognitive reordering that we can actively practice and facilitate, that likelihood increases further.[19]

Creative Systems Theory and the Application of a Creative Frame

We can arrive at a creative frame in multiple ways. As a start, we can consider what Integrative Meta-perspective teaches us about the workings of polarity. And we don't need the Creative Functions developmental picture to get there. I've described how culturally mature understanding "bridges" the polarized assumptions of times past. If we look closely, we recognize that polar relationships reflect an underlying symmetry. I've noted how polarities juxtapose some softer, we could say, more left-hand(or, to use language from psychology, more archetypally feminine) quality, with another quality that is harder, more right-hand (archetypally masculine). Creative Systems Theory describes how this basic symmetry is key to the workings of formative process. I've emphasized the important sense in which the relationship between the two

---

19   See Charles M. Johnston, MD, Hope and the Future: Confronting Today's Crisis of Purpose, ICD Press, 2018.

hands of any polarity, when understood, systemically becomes "procreative."

We get to a similar place if we shift our attention to intelligence. I've described how Integrative Meta-perspective makes it possible to better hold the whole of human intelligence, and I've observed Creative Systems Theory's claim that intelligence's multiplicity functions to support and drive formative process. Integrative Meta-perspective, just from where it takes us, thrusts us into a world in which the workings of intelligence are dynamic and systemic; and it does so in a whole new sense—we could say in a sense that is expressly creative.

A closer look at intelligence's multiplicity and its role in formative process helps fill out this creative picture. It also provides a glimpse into how Creative Systems Patterning in Time helps us understand change in human systems. Creative Systems Theory proposes that we are the uniquely creative creatures we are, not merely because we are conscious; but because of the ways that the various aspects of our intelligence work and the ways they work together. The theory describes how our various intelligences—or we might say, "sensibilities," to reflect all they encompass—relate in specifically creative ways. And it delineates how different ways of knowing and different relationships between ways of knowing predominate at specific times in any human change process. The way Creative Systems Theory ties the underlying structures of intelligence to patterns of change in human systems both helps us better understand change and hints at the possibility of better predicting it.

The theory argues that our various intelligences work together in ways that are both collaborative and creative. It describes how human intelligence is uniquely configured to support creative change by driving and facilitating its workings. Our various modes of intelligence, juxtaposed like colors on a color wheel, function together as creativity's mechanism. Like a Ferris wheel, it is continually turning, continually in motion. The way the various facets of intelligence juxtapose creates purposeful change, inherent to our natures.

During creativity's initial," incubation" stage, the dominant intelligence is the kinesthetic, "body" intelligence, if you will. It is like being pregnant but not quite sure with what; there is only an inner sensing that takes the form of "inklings" and faint "glimmerings.". If I find myself in this state and want to feed the creative process, I do things that help me to be reflective and to connect in my body. I might take a long walk in the woods, draw a warm bath, or build a fire in the fireplace.

Next comes creativity's "inspiration" stage, in which new possibility first comes into the light. The dominant intelligence here is the imaginal—that which defines art, myth, and the let's-pretend world of young children. The products of this stage of the creative process can appear suddenly— Archimedes's "Eureka"—or they may come more subtly and gradually. It is this stage, and this part of our larger sensibility, that we most traditionally associate with things creative.

With creativity's "perspiration" stage we give inspiration solid form. The dominant intelligence is different still: more emotional and visceral, the intelligence of heart and guts. It is here that we confront the hard work of finding the right approach and the most satisfying means of expression. We confront limits to our skills and challenge ourselves to push beyond them. The perspiration stage tends to bring a new moral commitment as well as emotional edginess. We must compassionately but unswervingly confront what we have created if it is to stand the test of time.

With creativity's "finishing and polishing" stage we give creation detail and engage the tasks of completion. Here, rational intelligence takes the more dominant role. More attentive to aesthetic precision than the periods previous, finishing and polishing is also more concerned with audience and outcome. It brings final focus to the creative work, its clarity of thought and nuances of style needed for effective communication.

While we might assume that the creative task is now done, we've in fact come at best half of the way, and the changes that mark the second half of the formative process are equally as important and transforming. During creation's second half, we step back from the work and appreciate it from a new perspective, where we can appreciate the relationship of the work to its creative contexts—both the context of ourselves and that of the time and place in which it was created. The result of this "seasoning" process is a more integrative picture, one in which the work becomes, in a new sense, "second nature." Specifically regarding intelligence, we combine our diverse ways of knowing more consciously, becoming better able to apply our intelligences in various combinations and balances as time and situation warrant. Through this process we engage the work as a whole and ourselves in relationship to it.

We can apply this progression to formative processes of all sorts. We see something similar whether our concern is an act of innovation, personal psychological development, or culture and its evolution. For example, we find the same bodily intelligence that orders creative "incubation" to play a prominent role in the infant's rhythmic world of movement, touch, and taste. The realities of early tribal cultures also draw deeply on body sensibilities. Truth in tribal societies is synonymous with the rhythms of nature; and, through dance, song, story, and drumbeat, with the body of the tribe.

The same imaginal intelligence that we saw ordering creative "inspiration" we find in the play-centered world of the young child. We also hear it voiced with particular strength in early civilizations such as ancient Greece or Egypt, the Incas and Aztecs in the Americas, or the classical East, with their mythic pantheons and great symbolic tales.

We find the same emotional and moral intelligence that orders creative "perspiration" occupying center stage in adolescence, with its deepening passions and pivotal struggles for identity. It can also be felt strongly in the beliefs and values of the European Middle Ages, times marked by feudal struggle and ardent moral conviction; and even today, where struggle and conflict seem to be forever recurring.

In a similar way, we find the same rational intelligence that powers the "finishing and polishing" tasks of creativity taking new prominence in young adulthood, as we strive to create our unique place in the world of adult expectations. This more refined and refining aspect of intelligence stepped to the fore culturally during the Renaissance and the Age of Reason; and, in the West, has held sway in modern times.

Finally, and of particular pertinence to the concept of Cultural Maturity, we find the same, more consciously integrative relationship to intelligence that we see in the "seasoning" stage of a creative act ordering the unique developmental capacities—the wisdom—of a lifetime's second half. In our current cultural stage, we can also see this same integrative relationship with intelligence just beneath the surface in the Western advances that have transformed understanding through the last century.

We associate the Age of Reason with Descartes's assertion that "I think, therefore I am." We could make a parallel assertion for each of these other cultural stages: "I am embodied, therefore I am"; "I imagine, therefore I am"; "I am a moral being, therefore I am"; and, if the concept of Cultural Maturity is accurate, "I understand maturely and systemically with the whole of myself, therefore I am." The concept of Cultural Maturity proposes that the words you have just read about intelligence's creative workings have made sense because such consciously integrative dynamics are beginning to reorder how we think and perceive.

Creative Systems Theory Patterning Concepts

I've observed how Creative Systems Theory includes three basic kinds of "patterning concepts." The first, Patterning in Time, addresses change in human systems. The chart in Figure A-3 summarizes Creative Systems Theory Patterning in Time observations as they pertain to common developmental processes: a simple creative act, individual human development, the growth of a relationship, and, of particular importance, the history of culture. It also indicates the language that the theory uses in making such distinctions: Pre-Axis for "incubation stage" sensibilities, Early-Axis for "inspiration stage" sensibilities, Middle-Axis for "perspiration stage" sensibilities, and Late-Axis for "finishing and polishing" stage sensibilities.

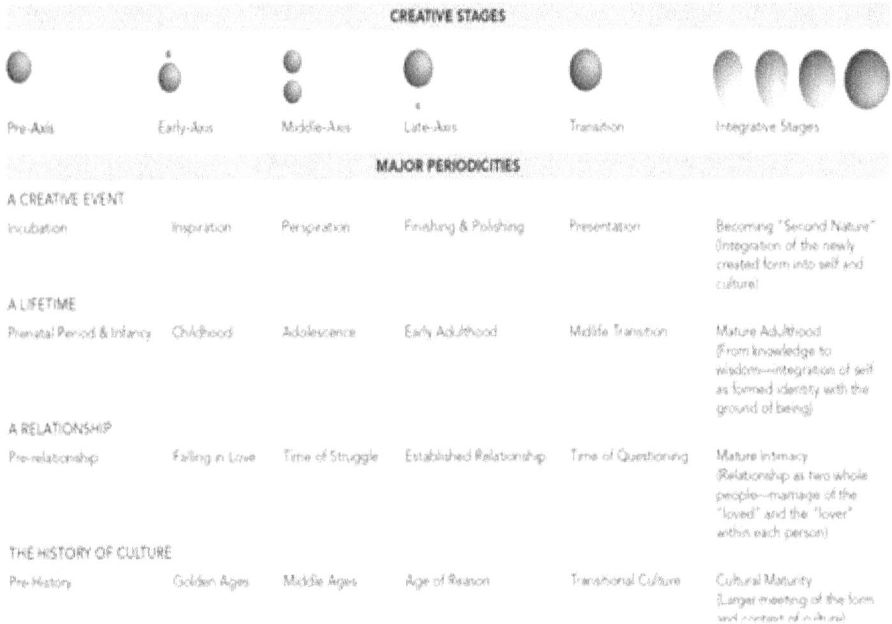

CREATIVE STAGES

Pre-Axis	Early-Axis	Middle-Axis	Late-Axis	Transition	Integrative Stages

MAJOR PERIODICITIES

A CREATIVE EVENT

Pre-Axis	Early-Axis	Middle-Axis	Late-Axis	Transition	Integrative Stages
Incubation	Inspiration	Perspiration	Finishing & Polishing	Presentation	Becoming "Second Nature" (Integration of the newly created form into self and culture)

A LIFETIME

Prenatal Period & Infancy	Childhood	Adolescence	Early Adulthood	Midlife Transition	Mature Adulthood (From knowledge to wisdom—integration of self as formed identity with the ground of being)

A RELATIONSHIP

Pre-relationship	Falling in Love	Time of Struggle	Established Relationship	Time of Questioning	Mature Intimacy (Relationship as two whole people—marriage of the "loved" and the "lover" within each person)

THE HISTORY OF CULTURE

Pre-History	Golden Ages	Middle Ages	Age of Reason	Transitional Culture	Cultural Maturity (Larger meeting of the form and content of a culture)

Fig. A-3. Formative Process from the Perspective of Creative Systems Theory

The second type of patterning concept, Patterning in Space, addresses here-and-now systemic differences. We can use Patterning in Space notions to help tease apart internal psychological mechanisms and to map the dynamics and interactions of interpersonal relationships, organizations, communities, nations, and the planet as a whole. The most filled-out and recognized Patterning in Space tool is the Creative Systems Personality Typology.

The third category of patterning concepts, what the theory calls Whole-Person/Whole-System, addresses attributes that are products of systems as entireties. Its notions focus on what truth at its most basic becomes with Cultural Maturity's cognitive reordering. Some examples include the concept of Aliveness, a general way of talking about possibility and motivation; the idea of Capacitance, a measure of overall human capacity; and the notion of Creative Symptoms, a way of thinking about protective mechanisms in human systems.

Creative Systems Theory Patterning concepts provide overarching perspective for understanding what makes us who we are and what good choices look like in today's world. They offer a comprehensive set of tools—applicable to both individuals and social systems—for making our way in a culturally mature reality.

The Dilemma of Trajectory and Transitional Absurdity

To make full sense of what we see in our times, a couple of further Creative Systems concepts require brief attention. The first, what Creative Systems Theory calls the Dilemma of Trajectory, describes how Cultural Maturity's changes involve more than just letting go of one cultural stage and moving to another, how they bring into question the whole developmental orientation that has previously defined growth and truth. The Dilemma of Trajectory makes changes like those that the concept of Cultural Maturity describes as inescapably necessary.

We can describe the Dilemma of Trajectory in multiple ways, but most simply by using the language of polarity. Creative Systems Theory delineates how each stage in culture to this point has been defined by greater distance between polar opposites and a greater emphasis on difference. (Whereas in tribal times, connectedness to nature and tribe was primary; today, materialism and individuality prevails.)

We can also frame the Dilemma of Trajectory in terms of intelligence's multiplicity. We evolved from times in which the more creatively germinal aspects of intelligence—the body and the imagination—most informed experience (to be part of a tribe was to know the tribal dances and rituals); to times in which the rational—with a limited contribution from the emotional— holds the much larger influence (enter the Age of Reason). We can also describe this evolution in terms of culture's story—how it has taken us from times in which archetypally feminine influences ruled to times in which the archetypally masculine is the defining presence.

In our time, this organizing trajectory has reached an extreme: Truth has come to be defined almost exclusively by difference (for example, we view objective and subjective as wholly separate worlds); we equate rationality with understanding; and extreme archetypally masculine values prevail (such as those of the marketplace and science). The Dilemma of Trajectory alerts us to the danger of going further in this direction. Indeed, in an important sense, that direction ceases to be an option: We would not do well if we lost what remaining connection we have with nature, our bodies, or the more receptive aspects of experience that form the basis of human relationships. Continuing our current trajectory would irretrievably alienate us from aspects of who we are that are essential to being human.

So what are we to do? We could go back—a proposal at least implied in certain kinds of social advocacy. But going back is not any more likely to get us where we need to go. Unless there is another option, the human experiment could be at an end. Fortunately, by reconciling the Dilemma of Trajectory, Integrative Meta-perspective offers a possible way forward, a way that points toward an essential kind of human realization and fulfillment.

An additional concept relates to an observation that could seem to prove the concept of Cultural Maturity wrong. Much in today's world appears opposite to that which the concept predicts; for example, increasing political and social polarization, widespread denial and refusal to set limits with regard to challenges such as climate change and the extinction of species, and the growing prevalence of authoritarian rule in places where we might have assumed it to be something of the past. Given that we find so much in contemporary human behavior that seems ludicrous—and often rather scary, it can be hard to believe that it is possible for the species to get any wiser.

It may not be. But it turns out that much of what we see is indeed consistent with the concept of Cultural Maturity. The concept predicts Transitional Absurdity, characterized not just by new possibilities, but also by times of regression and distorted ways of thinking.[20]

New Capacities and Critical Challenges

Creative Systems Theory argues that we will be able to address challenges ahead for the species—and in the process address the Dilemma of Trajectory and confront Transitional Absurdity—only to the degree we can apply the new human capacities that I've described, which follow from Cultural Maturity's cognitive reordering. Noting a few of those challenges and what they will ask of us helps clarify how this is so. With regard to better understanding personality style differences, in each case the more complete kind of self-awareness and the greater capacity for collaboration that comes with such understanding provides support for needed changes.

How can we act morally in a world without obvious moral guideposts? Until very recently, culture in its parental role provided us with clear moral rules; our task was simply to understand and obey those rules. Today, traditional moral guideposts are losing their authority and the moral relativisms that tend to replace them leave us feeling rudderless. We find ourselves in an

---

[20] I wrote the short book, Perspective and Guidance for a Time of Deep Discord: Why We See Such Extreme Social and Political Polarization—and What We Can Do About It (ICD Press, 2021) in response to some of today's particularly concerning Transitional Absurdities.

increasingly complex, change-permeated moral landscape. Cultural Maturity's cognitive changes offer that we might address moral questions with a new systemic depth and nuance, and with it a comfort with uncertainty and complexity that has not before been an option.

How do we keep from destroying ourselves? I've noted how collective identity through history has depended on dividing our worlds into "chosen people" and "evil others." This way of defining who we are is becoming increasingly problematic, with the nuclear genie now out of the bottle and terrorism an inescapable threat. Our safety in the long term will depend on bringing greater maturity and sophistication to how we understand our human differences and how we relate to conflict. Integrative Meta-Perspective's systemically encompassing vantage offers the possibility of getting beyond the polarized and polarizing assumptions that have created us-versus-them worlds.

How do we avoid making the planet unlivable? Climate change, global industrialization, and the broader effects of growing human population threaten to make existence on the planet increasingly unpleasant. It is quite possible that the earth will eventually become uninhabitable for us. If we are going to avoid such an outcome, we must step beyond our modern heroic mythology that views limits only as constraints to be overcome. Culturally mature perspective highlights the inherent role of limits in the workings of living systems and helps us engage them in the most creative ways.

Looking ahead, how will the requirements of effective leadership change? Today, trust in leadership is less than it was even at the height of anti-authoritarian rhetoric in the 1960s. We could easily assume—and people have argued—that this modern lack of confidence in leadership reflects something gone terribly wrong: broad failure on the part of leaders, a loss of moral integrity on the part of those being led, or even an impending collapse of society. If it does, there is little reason to have hope.

The concept of Cultural Maturity offers an explanation that is more optimistic but also more demanding. It alerts us to the fact that the meaning of leadership is changing— in all parts of our lives, from the leadership needed in ourselves to make good personal choices, to that required for effective leadership of organizations and nations. Along with altering the way we go about making decisions, these changes invite important reflection about possible next chapters in our thinking about governance and and our structuring of governmental institutions.

Leadership's new picture is not all positive. Today we reside in an awkward, in-between time regarding these changes. When we do see leadership that begins to reflect culturally mature capacities, people are as likely to attack it as celebrate it. But if the concept of Cultural Maturity is correct, moving forward in how we embody and relate to leadership is both possible and essential.

How will love change in times ahead? Love might seem more a personal concern, less pertinent to big-picture cultural well-being; but certainly the topic is relevant to people's sense of fulfillment. Changes we see today regarding love are also pertinent to what relationships of every kind will require of us in times ahead. Romantic love as symbolized by Romeo and Juliet represented a powerful step forward from what came before it—marriages arranged by one's family or a matchmaker. But it can't be the last chapter in love's story. While we idealize such love because it is based on individual choice, it was never ideal. Modern romantic love makes the other person our completion—our "white knight" or "fair maiden." Rather than love between whole people, it is "two-halves-make-a-whole" love. Today's challenge is to love as whole beings, and Integrative Meta-perspective makes Whole-Person love newly possible.[21] A related change is reordering relationships of every sort. In the end, these changes challenge us to rethink not only relationships, but the nature of

---

21   I examine this topic in depth in my book, On the Evolution of Intimacy: A Brief Exploration into the Past, Present, and Future of Gender and Love (ICD Press, 2019).

individual identity; and with this, what it means to choose and to live purposefully.

What will it mean to use technologies wisely in times ahead? Technological innovations will be key to future advancement. But if we are to have a healthy and survivable future, it is just as important that they more effectively assess their benefits and identify potential unintended consequences. These might seem like wholly technical tasks; but, in fact, carrying them out with the needed sophistication will require a maturity of perspective that we have not before been capable of. It has been our Modern Age tendency to treat technology as a god. If we continue to do so, our profound capacities as tool makers could eventually be our undoing. Culturally mature perspective helps us get beyond technological gospel thinking and bring the nuance of understanding needed to apply new technologies wisely.

How must we define progress if our actions are to successfully take us forward? In modern times, we have envisioned progress as an onward-and-upward trajectory of increasing individuality and material achievement. While this definition has served us well, it cannot continue, for multiple reasons. Beyond the fact that it is not environmentally sustainable, it should prove less and less successful at giving our lives purpose. Compelling pictures of advancement must consider the full measure of human needs—not just individual accomplishment and material accumulation; but also human relationships, creativity, the health of our bodies, our larger sense of connectedness in life, and much more.

Another critical reason, which I have just touched on, explains why our past definition of progress cannot continue to serve us. The Dilemma of Trajectory describes how continuing on as we have would sever us from attributes that are critical to who we are, to being human. If this conclusion is accurate, not only is clinging to progress's familiar definition unwise: Doing so is no longer an option. Our future depends on defining progress in more systemically complete ways.

As these multiple challenges make clear, like it or not, we live in times that ask a lot of us. But whatever the origins of today's increasingly demanding challenges, it is important to recognize that, with sufficient courage and persistence, Cultural Maturity works as an antidote.

Looking at the Evidence

Radical notions like Creative Systems Theory's application of a creative frame and the concept of Cultural Maturity require strong evidence. Here we've seen how CST's developmental framework—whether we approach it through the lens of polarity or through the evolution of intelligence—provides valuable conceptual perspective. In addition, the conclusion that something resembling the concept will be necessary is supported by the ability of Cultural Maturity's changes to make needed new capacities possible. Furthermore, notions like the Dilemma of Trajectory and Transitional Absurdity are consistent with a creative frame's predictions, and make the need for a concept similar to Cultural Maturity impossible to escape.

There is even more evidence in favor of the power of a creative frame. For example, in my overarching book, *Creative Systems Theory*, I describe how its application lets us answer questions that have always left us baffled, including many quandaries of the "eternal" sort. It turns out that we need Integrative Meta-perspective not just to answer such questions, but to ask them in helpful ways. Some examples that I touch on in the book: How do we reconcile the experience of free will with what logically seems a deterministic world? Are the beliefs of science and religion merely different, or do they represent parts of a larger picture? And how do we best understand the human species 'place in the larger scheme of things?

More specifically with regard to the concept of Cultural Maturity, for me the most compelling evidence that its thesis is correct is the simplest: I don't see another way of framing the human task that is consistent with a healthy and vital future. Indeed, I don't see another way of framing the human task that is ultimately survivable. Unless I have missed something important, Cultural Maturity becomes the only option going forward, the only game in town.

An observation implied in Creative Systems Theory's developmental picture provides further support for Cultural Maturity's significance, if it is correct: Cultural Maturity's changes may do more than provide an effective response to today's immediate challenges;. they may offer a basic blueprint for the right thought and action applicable far into humanity's future. We can think of Cultural Maturity's changes as ultimate human achievement.

INDEX

www.ingramcontent.com/pod-product-compliance
Lightning Source LLC
Chambersburg PA
CBHW060922140726
47996CB00001B/344